This is a working book! It's job is to
as possible with an fresh and inspir
You can help by:-

a) Reading the book and passing it
b) Passing it on right now if reading
c) Ordering your own copy, then pa
d) Giving us your feedback on the t

Record of this book's journey:-
Name........................... Town/City.................................

Order copies and gives us your feedback on:- book@grubb.org.uk

Leading Schools from Failure to Success

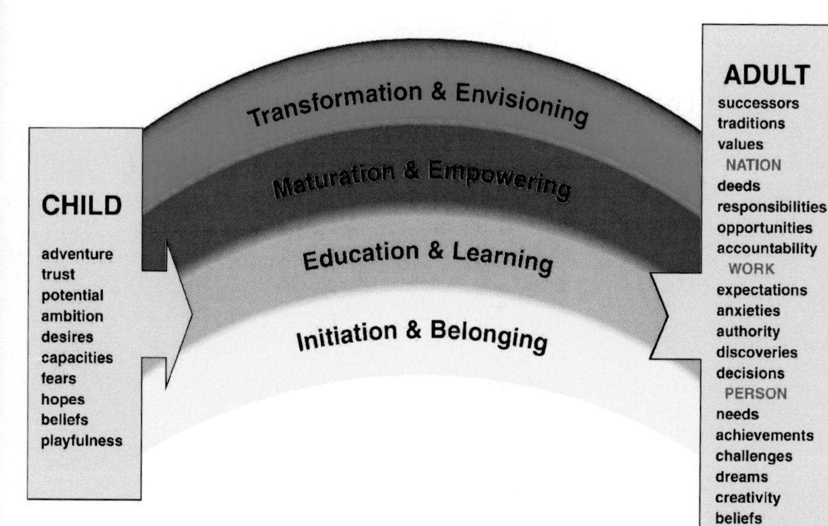

THE REED RAINBOW
of
Human and Social Development

Leading Schools from Failure to Success

How three Christian headteachers transformed church schools

John Bazalgette,
Bruce Reed, Ian Kehoe & Jean Reed

Foreword by
Lord Dearing

Commentary by
Dr Jill Clough

UIT CAMBRIDGE LTD.
CAMBRIDGE, ENGLAND

First published in England in 2006.
UIT Cambridge Ltd.
PO Box 145
Cambridge
CB4 1GQ
England

Tel: +44 1223 302 041
Web: www.uit.co.uk

10 9 8 7 6 5 4 3 2 1

13-digit ISBN 978-0-9544529-2-6
(10-digit) ISBN 0-9544529-2-5

Printed in Great Britain by Biddles Ltd,
King's Lynn, Norfolk

Contents

1 Vicious circle to virtuous circle **1**
1.1 Challenging circumstances 1
1.2 Initiating a virtuous circle 3
1.3 Three transformed church schools 3
1.4 Who ought to read this book 4

2 Learning to belong **7**
2.1 From failure to success 7
Three failing church schools are turned round . . 8
Transformation or change? 12
2.2 Making a school worth belonging to 12
Where children and young people want to belong 13
A place that the community wants to own 24
The result of enabling people to belong 44
BEING the head 50
The centrality of worship in these schools 57

3 Principles of Leadership **67**
3.1 Leadership of person 68
The background to our understanding 68
A working model of social development 68
Leading school transformation 81
Role as a process of self-disciplined behaviour . . 83
Transformative behaviour – power and authority . 88

3.2 Leading and managing systems 97
Working with experience 98
Concepts of 'person', 'system', 'context' and 'role' 100
3.3 The headteacher's leadership in transformation . 122
Inclusiveness in Church of England schools 123
The significance of worship in school life 127
3.4 Assembly and worship in community schools . . 128
A theory of religion in society 129
'Religion' in institutions 130
'Religion' in schools 131
Civil religion & Christian faith in schools 134

4 Implications **139**
4.1 Pupil leadership and school transformation 142
Leadership of the pupils 142
Leadership by the pupils 144
Preparing teachers for leadership by pupils 145
4.2 The formation of wise heads 146
Development for Governors 147
4.3 Being inclusive: gift and challenge 148

5 Lessons to be drawn: using free resources **151**

Appendix: the study method outlined **153**
Notes **155**
Glossary **159**

About the Authors **161**

Foreword
by Lord Dearing

This study is first about the way three newly appointed head teachers went about transforming three failing Church of England schools, whilst retaining the staff already in post and drawing pupils from the same disadvantaged catchment areas. Very down to earth stuff some of it; for example what the head did when some pupils trashed the toilets; but also memorable for the way their courage and faith shone though their work in the schools. It shows how the heads worked with pupils who had been disruptive, resistant to learning and ready to play truant at the first excuse, and led them to become active agents in their own school's transformation.

The first part of the book is based on discussions with the heads, their staff, pupils, parents and governors, who each contributed comments on the heads as they saw them from their individual standpoints.

In the second part, the book distils from this, and from their own experience, the underlying principles of leadership. I valued that, because from my own experience I know that very different people can be successful leaders, and that in leadership they were true to their own personalities, but who in succeeding had things in common. This second part is about these things the heads had in common as they discharged their roles as a leader. I would underline the words, 'a leader' here, because central to success is engaging others in the transformation, and becoming themselves leaders and agents of change.

Once challenged myself to address senior executives on leadership, I recall saying, it was the art of getting other people to want very much to work with you towards the goals you had identified in consultation with them. But as this study brings out, there is much more to it than that.

The book is specifically about the practice of three Christians, as it happens none of them Anglicans, coming into schools where perhaps only a quarter of the staff might be described as practising Christians. They were up front in declaring their faith, introducing prayer into staff meetings and using assemblies for reflection and worship rather than the running of the school. This was part of their being true to themselves and drawing strength from their faith.

But this is a study that I would commend to anyone taking on the professional challenge of 'mending' a failing school. A deeply held faith may provide a 'turbo-charging' factor, but the practice and principles are the same for all of us. Although the analytical section makes demands of the reader, I would particularly commend it because it invites reflection. Indeed, I wish I had had such a text to read before taking my own first major leadership role, for to be honest I gave little structured thinking to how I would do the job. While looking back I can see that I did some things rights, I could have been more effective if I had – as the writers of this book do – committed myself to thinking through how best to achieve my aims, and in particular how best to engage all the other players, and especially some of the disaffected, disillusioned element, in the achievement of my aspirations.

The writers, in noting that these three Church schools had an inclusive admissions policy in taking pupils of other faiths and no faith, go beyond their immediate remit, to argue a case for such a policy by all Church of England schools, in educational terms, and as making a contribution to the health and well being of local communities. This is already the practice of most Church of England schools, but we may hear more about that issue in the year ahead.

I am also clear that the issue of responding to the needs of pupils in failing schools will also be increasingly on the agenda.

In both these senses this is a timely book, but in reflecting on it, the words that will remain with me were those of a pupil, who when invited to comment on what motivated the Head, said, it was that he was 'doing it for them'. Not a bad recommendation!

Surbiton, September 2005

Editor's Note

The publishers gratefully acknowledge the generous support of **The National Society** and of **The Jerusalem Trust** in publishing this book.

The book is based on research which was aided by a grant from **The National College for School Leadership** to the Church of England Board of Education.

Introduction

This book gives a gripping account of how three church schools facing challenging circumstances improved. Unlike so many other books and articles on this topic the authors look beyond the action plans and innovative practice to examine what drives all of those responsible for the improvement.

The authors examine, within the context of the three church schools investigated, the concept of moral purpose. The authors relate this directly to the Christian tradition; however it is important to note that the messages are applicable to all of those concerned with school improvement regardless of their own faith or that of the school community.

Teacher educators and governments are grappling with trying to ensure the next generation of teachers can prepare students to work in ways in which we cannot yet imagine. This book is a timely reminder that the next generation of teachers need to understand how to create a school ethos by which the whole school community works together to support and challenge each other.

Gary Phillips
Headteacher
Lilian Baylis Technology School
London

Chapter 1

Turning a vicious circle into a virtuous one

1.1 Challenging circumstances

The government has a way of talking about certain schools: they call them 'schools facing challenging circumstances'. These schools have a cluster of 'circumstances' which they face. These include all or some of the following:

- *A stereotyped negative image* of the school in the local community which may bear little relation to reality – the pupils are spoken of as 'difficult, rowdy, truants, destructive and resistant to learning'; the teachers are parodied as 'weak, uninterested in their pupils, showing low levels of competence, disconnected from the real world'; the headteacher is seen as inept (probably politically motivated) and the buildings are described as unkempt and litter-ridden.
- *Poor achievement* in examinations such as SATs* and GCSE is widely spoken about.

*A glossary is provided at the end of the book explaining the acronyms which are in common use in educational circles.

- *Low morale* across the school is a consequence, with depressed teachers, high levels of staff sickness, absenteeism and high turnover; truancy amongst the children; troublesome pupils who are subject to regular short-term or permanent exclusions; listless governors and frustrated headteachers.

- *A depressed intake* of pupils results, with low levels of literacy and numeracy on entrance which reinforces the negative image, and leads to difficulties in recruiting and holding on to good staff.

- *Angry parents* who protest at their children being sent to the school against their wishes.

- *A local education authority* (LEA) which becomes more and more anxious and active in promoting remedies based more on sanctions which include threats of the removal of the Governing Body and even closure.

When an Ofsted report exposes real problems to public scrutiny, local papers have a field day with 'original' headlines like 'Local school caned', which reinforce the vicious circle. In the worst case, the local education authority may be minded to sack the governing body and administer the school itself. It becomes increasingly difficult to differentiate fact from fiction and the situation quickly goes from bad to worse.

Authors' Comment: This is not just an imaginary picture. One of us has been a governor of a school which went through exactly this cycle, including being 'named and shamed' by the Secretary of State for Education, having a running battle for five years with some of its local authority officers, going through five heads in five years and having the school vilified openly by a senior national politician who had never had anything to do with the school.

1.2 Initiating a virtuous circle

There are several characteristic actions taken to try to break out of a vicious circle.

The first action is to appoint a new head, perhaps parachuting in a 'super head' on a short-term contract. The new head is given the backing to clear out the poor staff and recruit new, bright-eyed and bushy-tailed ones. Such heads search high and low for good publicity (and suppress the bad); they may wine and dine the local newspaper editors to get them to change their attitude towards the school. Their intention is to transform the intake to the school: the poorly performing teachers, badly behaved children are removed and places refused to those excluded from other schools. The hope is to fill vacant places with eager, learning-oriented youngsters, so a campaign may be mounted towards primary school heads to encourage them to send their brighter, better children to the school. The new head probably builds in new systems of rewards and punishments; she (or he) is likely to set in train a professional development process to build up the staff.

However, if the vicious circle is well embedded in the local community even the very best laid plans still go astray.

But if the head succeeds and then decides to move on in their career, the question is raised: will the change hold or will the school slide back into the same old vicious circle again? Was the change really a function of the personality of that head or did a real organizational transformation take place that can survive? A sad question arising from being successful in transforming a school: is that head now condemned to a life sentence in that school?

1.3 Three transformed church schools

This book is about three examples of schools being transformed, not just temporarily but permanently, with only one change of 'personnel': the headteacher. Otherwise the staff were unchanged and the pupil intake remained the same. All three were schools whose morale was rock bottom, test and exam results were far below acceptable levels, they were problems to their local education authorities and an embarrassment to their dioceses. All three schools moved from being the most unpopular schools in their area to becoming over-subscribed; from being rated by Ofsted as schools needing Special Measures to being rated as improving schools, demonstrated by good standards of teaching in classrooms, rising exam results and falling disciplinary difficulties.

The action that led to their turning the corner in each case was the appointment of a new headteacher, a person for whom their Christian faith was a core part of their understanding of the meaning of life and the call to work in these particular schools; none of them saw their task as being to evangelize anyone else. They each felt that they had been called to a special mission which they expected to unfold as they worked with the existing teachers, children, parents and governors of their school.

This book is about the principles that each of them intuitively applied in their work. It sets out to describe those and to show that while their Christianity was an important factor – perhaps a turbo-charging factor – they worked on the basis of a professionalism that can underlie all good headship. We set out to describe those principles so that others can assess their practice against them and, where they feel they might be useful, adopt them for themselves.

However, while their faith was an important factor for them, what they did provides examples of good practice for any professional head, whatever their own belief or personal philosophy.

1.4 Who ought to read this book

This book is based on experience that has been reflected on and thought about. It is *not* an academic treatise. The lives of children, men and women come alive in it: what they show is a new perspective on school experience which is practical and down to earth. What we describe is how schools were transformed –

repaired may be a better word, since no-one starts out by wanting to be involved in a bad school. From the practice of these schools, practical principles have been drawn out which can be put to work through a new mind-set, costing very little in cash terms.

We have written this book with the following people in mind: the ambitious head who wants to go further; the head who is in a mess; the aspiring head (i.e. a senior teacher or deputy who wants to make a difference where they are but also wants to impress an interview panel); governors who want to get to grips with their school; National College of School Leadership Consultant Leaders who want texts to recommend to those consulting to them.

We also think that Bishops, Diocesan Directors of Education and their senior staff in both the Church of England and the Roman Catholic churches will want to read it because of the section about worship in schools.

Organizations such as the National Association of Head Teachers and the Association of School and College Leaders (formerly the Secondary Heads Association) will find value in it. The heads and governors of independent schools may benefit from it.

Those colleges and university departments of education where school leadership and management are high on their teaching list, both with undergraduates and with those studying for Masters and PhDs, are likely to want to have it available. Those general departments of management in universities that want something that comes from left field will be interested.

Chapter 2

Learning to belong

2.1 From failure to success

This is essentially the story of three church schools that were turned from failure to success. They were schools with a history of poor performance going back several years, schools which those responsible for them wanted to get rid of: after several 'fresh starts', one was transferred from local authority control to the local Anglican diocese; in another, the governors had been lobbying the diocese to hand the school over to the local education authority (which the authority was not enthusiastic about); in the third school, the local authority and the diocese had decided to have one last serious try at saving it before giving in to what seemed like inevitable closure. All three were subject to severe criticism from Ofsted and had been either in Special Measures or designated as having serious weaknesses: all three were schools that aroused widespread concern about their educational effectiveness.

The following sections describe factually the successes and achievements in these three schools. We write about their kinds of pupils – which were different in each, though in all three they had been unpopular schools with parents. We tell about the new heads: they were experienced professionals (one was already an experienced head) and they were all practising Christians. The staffs of all three schools remained broadly unchanged and the profile of the intakes remained as they had been. The head was the only new factor in each situation. To clarify our thinking, we differentiate between 'change' (all schools change all the time as, year by year, new children join and others leave) and 'transformation' where the spirit of a school changes.

Three failing church schools are turned round

Achievements

In the first school, three years after the new head had been appointed, Ofsted commented on it clearly being an *'improving school. The confidence of parents and primary schools has been won back.'* The pupil roll had increased from 556 and falling fast, to a roll of 677 and the school was now oversubscribed. Good GCSEs were achieved by 30% of pupils against 21% previously. Absence had dropped substantially with unauthorized absence falling from 11% to 1%. Staying on and going to college or on to training was up to 74%. In 2002, a grant of £1.9m was made for the development of a new sports hall, language department and learning resources area.

In the second school, good GCSEs were achieved by 42% of pupils in 2001, compared with 25% in 1997. The pupil roll had risen to 757 in 2001 (from a dwindling 500 six years before) with 167 applicants for every 100 places in the school. Attendance had risen from 88.4% to 91% over two years and unauthorized absence had fallen to 0.7%.

We studied the third school at the point two years after the new head took over, so there was less time to bring things round. However, improved pupil behaviour meant that fixed term exclusions had dropped from 1011 days shared between 138 pupils in 1999 to 64 shared by seven pupils in 2002. Permanent exclusions had fallen from six to nil over the same period. The visit of Her Majesty's Inspectors (HMI) in 2000 found that nine out of ten lessons were satisfactory, with over half being rated good or very good. This contrasted with the visit in the previous year where four out of ten lessons were deemed to be unsatisfactory. Major funds had been forthcoming to build a new technology block and community sports hall.

The schools before the new headteachers were appointed

The pupil intakes of all three schools were broadly similar. They had low levels of literacy and numeracy on entrance, with one school receiving 24% of its new pupils who were four years behind their chronological age; they all had high levels of special educational needs (between 24% and 54%); eligibility for free school meals ranged between 22% and 30%; one of the schools had 50% of its pupils coming from Sikh families, speaking English as an additional language; of the other two, one had a Muslim intake of about 10% of its pupils, while the third was almost entirely white Anglo-Saxon in its intake.

In all three schools there was a large body of staff who had been there for a long time. In the two schools that were already church schools, less that 25% were practising Christians, about another 25% were nominally so, while the remainder claimed no particular religious affiliation. In the school that had been a local authority school, there was a major fear about becoming a church school with many staff worried that their religious position would be put under pressure.

All three schools served communities that were disadvantaged in one way or another. Two of them served inner city areas from which the traditional industries and occupations had moved away. The other served an old housing estate which was separated from the affluent local town by a wide marsh and which contained many of the social problems associated with old-style estates: overcrowding, unemployment, fragmenting families, poverty and crime were commonplace. All of the schools suffered from poor morale, buildings that were deteriorating, parents who did not want their children to go to the school in question but who had been given no option, and teaching staff who felt defeated and had lost hope.

As happens so often, the local papers enjoyed attacking the schools, hunting out stories that could show the school in a bad light and, as we have already said, when Ofsted reports were published, revelling in the 'school gets caned' type of headline. As many schools in challenging circumstances know, the local press find that stories attacking the weaknesses of schools in their community help circulation, so their slant on the school is very hard to shift since critical stories are easy to come by, even about moderately good schools.

The single new factor

What is remarkable with these three transformed Church of England schools is that only one thing changed: the headteacher.

The two men became heads for the first time; the one woman was an experienced head who came to the school from the private sector. Otherwise, the profile of the pupil intake of all three schools was unchanged and the bulk of the staff stayed the same. In cases elsewhere where failing schools have been transformed, the common practice has been to make every effort to recruit new staff, to export the bulk of the existing teachers as soon as possible, and to try to change the intake profile.

Authors' Comment: Alongside the study on which this book is based, a small sub-study of three transformed community schools was done. In all three, the new heads had mounted a major clear out of existing staff, which had been done with more or less acrimony, along with a serious campaign to change the school's pupil profile.

These three heads themselves had three things in common, two of which would have been evident on their appointment and one of which could only emerge as they went about the job:

1. Though teaching in Anglican schools, *none of them was an Anglican*: two were Roman Catholics and one was a member of a Free Church. It so happened that all three of them came to their new posts from Roman Catholic schools.

2. As they took up the reins in their schools it became clear that they were *competent education professionals*: they fully understood what it meant to work in classrooms and the conditions that are necessary for pupils and teachers to succeed in that environment. The experienced head was already a competent professional in the role of head; the two who were new to headship showed that they were able to develop the skills and attitudes necessary to the job, based on their competence in the classroom.

3. They were all *secure and committed in their Christian faith.* They were not simply 'churchgoers', but their faith was woven into their lives so that issues about love, truth, justice, mercy, forgiveness and grace were features of their own lives and were influences upon the kind of leadership they offered to children and adults around them. They did not set out to proselytize or to convert their pupils to Christianity, but worked inclusively with all those associated with their schools.

None of them would call themselves 'super heads', though head hunters were after them to take up the challenge of other failing schools even before the changes they had introduced in their own schools had been properly bedded in.

While each of them was a person of strong character, ready and able to make a commitment to the task in front of them, none of them would believe that what they did was solely due to themselves as individuals. This is not to take anything away from them, but what the study showed was the essential elements of headship which can be developed with appropriate training and attention to formation.

We will describe what these three heads actually did, how that was experienced by others and what effect it had on the school. We will go on to explore the contribution of their Christian faith to the kind of leadership they exercised. At the end, we outline actions which can take these principles further, not only in failing schools, but in any school seeking to enhance its service to children and their local communities.

Transformation or change?

It is important to clarify to the reader that we make an important differentiation between 'transformation' and 'change'. The arrival of a new headteacher is a change just as every year a new intake of children, with everyone moving up a year and a cohort leaving is a change; but none of these means that the school has been transformed. By 'transformation' we mean that there is a shift in the culture and ways of being which result in different outcomes from the work of the school. If the transformation is positive, children achieve more, teachers function at new and higher levels of professionalism, parents are more satisfied with what is happening to their children and so on. Transformation can also be negative: these schools had all seen better days ten or more years before, but things had slipped and bad practice, poor professionalism, and low morale had taken over.

The key question is, what is needed to enable transformation to be sustained or embedded? Is there an 'X Factor' attached to the person of the head or is there more to it? If there is more, where the head is the single change, how does that person pass on a vision of the school and an understanding of the structures necessary to enable others in the school to sign up to the same enterprise, in its own real context? This includes parents and others who live and work in the area, as well as the structures that engage with the school such as the local education authority (LEA) and – in the case of church schools – the diocese.

We are thinking about three examples of transformation in the study we describe here. Hopefully, what we say will convey the underlying principles on which transformation came about in all three instances.

2.2 Making a school worth belonging to: features of transforming headship

To understand what these three headteachers had done we studied in depth their ways of working and its impact upon their colleagues, both children and adults. Just as a grain of dye is dropped into a flask of water and slowly the whole colour of the contents change, we planned to trace out what the changes in these schools were, beginning from the introduction of that new grain. We fill out the detail of how we did it in the Appendix.

Where children and young people want to belong

We have argued elsewhere that the most significant organizational relationship in a school is the covert one between the head and *all* the pupils. The head may not know all the children personally, but all the pupils will know the head and have feelings about them. Those feelings may be positive or negative, affecting the whole climate and culture of the school.

Experienced heads over many years have conveyed to us how they recognize that they are visible and 'known' to everyone in the school. This affects their behaviour when they meet anyone, since they feel in their bones that whenever they meet someone it is important to convey that the person is 'known' to them – as pupil, teacher, parent and so on. This is not to dissemble, but to consciously collect data of every kind, scrappy and comprehensive, which can be drawn upon so that children, teachers, support staff, parents and others from outside feel that the head has an awareness of them and their likely concerns.

It also means always behaving in ways that are experienced as communicating symbolic messages across the school. For example, a head who spots some litter may pick it up and invite a nearby student to dispose of it: how they do it could convey a message about being fellow members of a community concerned to keep it presentable, or as a 'superior being' giving an order to a subordinate. These small things say many things about the head, the student and the schools as a whole, which can be emulated by anyone else.

Care for pupils by itself is insufficient to transform relationships in a school

Care can simply make pupils feel comfortable and unchallenged. All three of these headteachers considered that true caring involved challenging pupils to perform to the level of their abilities, something which had been lacking in their schools before their arrival. The heads spoke about this, but so did their pupils and staff.

She is a very strong person but also a caring and loving person. **Pupil**

They allow you to succeed. ... He's the main person here. ... He tries to sort things for us ... There's the discipline factor; he's tough. There was no more menacing, no more nicking lunch money. **Ex-pupil**

He presents a caring and supportive attitude and invites interaction with others. He actively discourages bad behaviour but rewards pupils who strive to achieve their goals. **Parent**

The heads recognized the importance of this attitude themselves:

I saw caring as vigorous caring. I am seen as tough because I care. Care goes with challenge. **Headteacher**

When I came it was a caring Christian community now it has become a challenging Christian community. **Headteacher**

But sometimes there were other reactions which pose questions about the extent to which this firmness was recognized by everyone. As one pupil, perhaps looking for even greater discipline than the head was providing, remarked:

He seems not to want to create waves. He forgives too easily; he is not firm enough. **Pupil**

The working hypothesis about why this kind of care and challenge are present together in these particular schools is as follows. They had been generally seen as fragile because they were failing, yet this fragility did not deter the headteachers taking a disciplined approach because their experience of Christian faith enabled them to experience God's tough love for their own mistakes. They were prepared to forgive pupils in their weaknesses so that they would be restored and able to keep on trying – which is not the same as letting them off. Heads and teachers with other beliefs and philosophies will be able to name the touchstones that underpin their approach to the transformation of schools. As will be seen as the reader follows this account, there is ample ground for joint exploration between different philosophies and faiths through which to enhance the opportunities offered to children through their schools.

Take an example from two other schools, not in this study and not being church schools. A head put a misbehaving boy in a lunch time detention because of a misdemeanour committed in front of her. Realizing that by doing so she would deprive him of his lunch, she gave him her own sandwiches. In another school, a boy was taken to the head for continuously failing to come to school in school uniform trousers. Having taken him to task for his failure, the head realized that more needed to be done. Recognizing that the boy's family were in poor circumstances, the head took him to Asda and bought him a suitable pair, paying for them from his own pocket and telling the boy that he was not to broadcast this around the school.

Respect and belief in pupils' ability to respond

Even though many of them were disadvantaged and disruptive, the pupils were seen by the heads as having real worth, despite their previous negative effects on the school. This attitude, which was widely recognized, showed itself in the love the headteachers had for all their pupils, and was a key factor in turning around their behaviour and attitude to learning.

> *He seems to know all of us personally and he concentrates on people's good points and gives us a lot of praise.* **Pupil**

Jill Clough comments: Often a headteacher may not know as much as they would like. The chances are that they will have read reports about a pupil, heard remarks about them, noted previous interactions as much as they could. This can provide a strong intuitive sense of the potential of many of the pupils. Taking one's natural capacity seriously, developing as strong a sense of the potential of as many pupils as one can, enables a head to draw on that subconscious background when encountering a pupil. One may not immediately grasp their name but if they have a feeling that one has an awareness of them in the school on their terms, pupils will feel known and valued. If the pupils sense that the head is solely concerned for the school as an institution rather than for them as human beings who belong to it, the transaction has little meaning for them as pupils.

The headteacher saw pupils for what they are which did not blind him to what they did. Other people were not able to look at them in this way and called them rubbish. **Teacher**

Students like the small award schemes and certificates and merits introduced by the head. It gives pupils something to work a little bit harder for. They work harder because of the general feel-good factor now in place in the school. **Support staff**

He is always positive about the children, stressing they are essentially good and worthy of respect in a Christian context. This is clearly related to his own personal faith. **Teacher**

The head is interested in the welfare of all his pupils. He talks to them, knows their names, is seen around the school during lesson times and breaks. He is always ready to listen to them, whatever the problem. He very rarely raises his voice! **Support staff**

He emphasizes all the time that every child is precious. They can make a mistake and you forgive them. The head can be furious but forgiveness is there. **Governor**

The heads had views about this themselves:

We are proud of working with disadvantaged children.
Headteacher

We have changed the pastoral system in the school from being a benevolent one to being a loving one. It's about doing right for the individual and not just coping with them. **Headteacher**

The significance of the headteacher's belief

While this attitude towards the children would be found in many heads who do not have a Christian faith, these heads' capacity to look deeper into these deprived and rebellious pupils was related to their own experience of God. Their relationship with God was exemplified in their attitude towards their pupils' behaviour, *'you can deny the sin, but not the child'*. Forgiveness was there because of their experience of the personal love and forgiveness of God. They appreciated the costliness to God of forgiveness and also to themselves, as they in turn forgave. Their own awareness of 'new life' gave them confidence that their pupils could also change, so as headteachers they could really believe in them.

Jill Clough comments: It becomes very important to be able to say to pupils, 'I'm sorry; I got that wrong about you.' Such comments need to be used judiciously but honestly. This opens up one of the ways of liberating pupils to forgive one another. It creates a climate in the school where anyone – adult or child – is entitled to get things wrong, linking that with accepting one's action and seeking to make amends.

Parents and governors appreciated this behaviour from the headteachers, but in particular it put the staff under considerable pressure to decide how and whether to back him/her up and/or to follow it through. They had reason to experience as staff the same respect from their headteacher. Because they needed to be strong to do this, many had difficulties if they did not have the same belief in pupils, which is not itself a 'Christian' belief. What was clear, as we shall see later, was that they did not feel any pressure from the heads to adopt the head's own faith position.

Pupils began to believe in themselves

From a state of low self-esteem and poor opinions of one another, which led to bullying, the pupils gained a sense of self-worth and respect for one another. As a result, each school became a better and safer place.

> *Before it was like a dread to come to school but now it's OK.* **Pupil**

> *Before the head came everything was a mess. I hated school, I actually left the school I was bullied so much. Since I came back in Year 8 I have felt so much happier. Bullying has been cracked down.* **Pupil**

> *Pupils get noticed for their talents!* **Pupil**

> *I believe most students are motivated to work better because the teachers want to teach the pupils. I think this is down to the headteacher as I know he has meetings with staff every morning.* **Pupil**

Jill Clough comments: Close contact between head and staff, formal and informal, is of the highest importance. The day of the distant head, excluded from the staff room and only met on formal business, is no longer functional. The head communicates messages through her vocabulary, her way of speaking to staff, how she dresses, her punctuality and her general dependability. Through all these signifiers, the head defines a certain frame and encourages – indeed permits – staff to work within it themselves, because she shapes how the inner life and the external context of the school are seen.

School has become a place to work hard and play hard. **Pupil**

The pupils haven't 'succeeded' yet, but there is a move in the right direction. The atmosphere in the school has enabled people to feel safe. It is no longer out of control. There is a peer support system in the school which has improved the bullying and changed the culture. It has moved from being a victim school. **Teacher**

He makes it quite clear what is expected of them, in uniform/ discipline/ attitude etc, there is therefore an improvement in self-worth. **Parent**

Prefects have had their status improved, he has given them a sense of ownership. Pupils want to be prefects. **Teacher**

There is a sense of loyalty pervading the school, and pride. I think the pupils feel included because they are consulted and they have seen the improvements happen which benefited them. **Teacher**

The safety experienced by pupils was the result of headteachers being decisive about their control of the school's organization after consulting with staff and pupils. The heads themselves bore the anxiety and the risk of things getting out of hand, but simultaneously they set up procedures through which pupils could freely consult their tutors and senior managers about their problems. Therefore, the bullying itself was reduced because pupils no longer needed to take their bewilderment and anxiety out on each other.

Jill Clough comments: Staff, teachers and support staff, need to know that it is part of their real work to spend time listening to students. Continuously telling all staff that listening time is important time, as important as the time when they are directly teaching or doing other work, changes priorities so that pupils feel real and feel valued. Children will not talk to people who they feel are in a rush. Heads need to be imaginative in devising procedures that work in their school to safeguard listening time.

The pupils would not have had this protective relief if staff had not also experienced reduction in their own anxiety, owing to the headteacher's leadership and management. They could now follow the procedures for staff/pupil consultation with confidence, feeling that they owned them and their purpose rather than having them imposed on them.

The headteachers' motivation is recognized by the pupils as being centred on them

The concern to deliver high-quality education derived from the head's understanding of pupils and the pupils' needs, rather than by reference to their own professional career prospects. This is why they were prepared to take the risk of becoming headteachers of failing schools. They saw that a belief in education really meant working with children to develop their various capacities in their growth towards adulthood, when they could contribute to the well-being of society as citizens.

When asked what they thought the Head's motivation was, a group of students responded instantaneously, 'us'.

Group of pupils

The head looks after the pupils' needs rather than his own. **Pupil**

Even from an early stage, pupils were better motivated because they had more respect from the head. The pupils stopped making personal criticism of the head. He listens to them and they believe that he is doing things for their good. **Teacher**

My motivation is my belief that the children only have one chance.

Headteacher

> *If you are rooted in education, you need experience but know what you can do and what you cannot do. You are there to educate the whole pupil. Be very clear on your basis. Show by example it is something for others to respect.* **Diocesan adviser**

Obviously, other headteachers put the interests of their pupils before their own careers, but these headteachers did so because they saw their pupils in the light of God's purpose as Creator, that they become whole human beings. For them, this focus was not an option, it was a vocation to which they were called by God. It was the merit of these headteachers that they had the competence and breadth of vision to enable them to see the purpose of their schools as being able to produce more than short-term measurable results, however necessary they may be.

A major test was how long headteachers would continue at their present schools and what would cause them to move, since they have already gained recognition as being capable of rescuing schools. How will they handle the tension between pursuing their own careers and their concern for the well-being and futures of their current pupils? Already they were being headhunted, but remained committed to those children and adults.

Insistence by the headteachers that truth and reality are key to the relations between themselves and pupils

This influenced all the other relationships between pupils and pupils, and staff and pupils. It was built on the assumption that people will make mistakes and when this occurs it is more important to tell the truth; to make a mistake is less of a problem than to tell a lie. As people learned to take responsibility for their own behaviour and to face the consequences, this led to a 'no-blame' culture. Headteachers can only work with mistakes constructively if they are dealing with the realities of the situation.

Jill Clough comments: One implication of this for their work with staff is related to the head's capacity to give people authority to lead and manage within the sub-systems of the school, while still holding them accountable for what happens. This means that the head conveys that everyone is entitled to try things out and make mistakes: this opens up the idea of the 'honest mistake' which is recognized by all those involved who seek together to find a way to deal with the consequences. The antithesis of this is that the head has either to tell people what to do in detail or go about doing it themselves. If working with the truth is the normal way of behaving in the school, then all sorts of resources are released and real transformation can take place; but working with reality begins with the head.

What I have sought to develop here is the ability to be yourself and to be vulnerable ... Admit your mistakes, we're all beggars helping each other to find bread ... My experience is of my own Christian salvation. I am in need of forgiveness and I've found the person who forgives me; so I have nothing to fear; I have no fear of failure. **Headteacher**

I called a sudden end of afternoon assembly one day because the newly refurbished lavatories had been trashed. I harangued them for half-an-hour and told them this is a different kind of school and there are values which have been broken and you are all responsible. I expect the truth and I expect those who did it to come forward or if you know who did it to come and tell me ... The trick is to make a decision. You know if you do the right thing, the right thing will result. People will have to find faith in you. If you love children you can communicate that and teachers will come on line, and deep down that is why they are in it. You have to talk to children in the right way and do what you say. I know this is hugely important from when I was teaching. **Headteacher**

Jill Clough comments: In situations such as this one, the head must keep clearly in mind the human needs of everyone working in the school. In punishing the children in this instance, the head may close the damaged toilets, but there must be sufficient facilities available for everyone in the school to relieve themselves, even if this involves making suitable arrangements for opening some staff toilets to children. In another school, after a major water fight the head realized that to remove access to water would be inhumane so other sanctions had to be found. In these ways the values described in the quotation are lived out.

The behaviour system is an act of grace. **Headteacher**

Through the headteacher, there has been a definite move to the way we deal with staff and incidents, we are trying to approach everything based on Christian values. The headteacher says condemn the sin not the child, he looks for truth and justice. E.g. if a child is caught doing wrong and lies about it, the headteacher goes for the lying which is the worse sin, because everybody makes mistakes and you can face them together but not if the student is lying about it. The headteacher lives his values: he says to staff this is not a blame culture. You don't become a Christian school overnight. We are on a mission to be a Christian, Church school. **Senior teacher**

The behaviour management system is exceptional. It is higher than I've seen anywhere else (and I've been a head of three schools myself). Good behaviour is rewarded and bad behaviour is handled consistently and speedily. This is true across the whole staff. There is a theology underpinning what he does. I call it 'spiritual anthropology'. It's the belief in the nature of human beings: they need to know about high standards of right and wrong. ... This depends on an understanding of redemption and the possibility of forgiveness. **Diocesan Director of Education**

When people are trusted to tell the truth then the need for a blame culture decreases. Where there is also repentance for mistakes and failures, blame disappears as people discover they are in a position to learn from their mistakes. If they own their mistakes, the risk of implementing this *truth culture* is possible where headteachers were working with their own personal experience of truth, repentance and forgiveness from God. In the schools in question, the head's relation with pupils was not only one of truth, but also one of hope. Where headteachers consistently took this position and backed up others to do the same, it established telling the truth as a fundamental school value.

This value would be undermined if the headteacher's example were not followed by that of senior managers and staff. It was a vital test of the quality of leadership which the headteacher offered as to whether it permeated all school relationships, so that what was *said* about getting at the truth was backed by what was *done*.

Jill Clough comments: In some circumstances the recognition that the head's word is a bond may appear to be artificial. He may have to set up small scale events that draw attention to the issue: 'I said I would see you and I want to see you now' – 'I said I would write to your mother: has she received my letter?' and so on. In this way the dependability of the head and of the school as an institution are underlined.

A place where adults want to belong and which the community wants to own

Schools are complex places with mixed members: though they are set up by statute for the benefit of children, they are also places where adults earn their living. Unless they too feel the school is worth belonging to, teachers can come to feel trapped by their economic and other needs, which can lead to the deterioration of their commitment and capacity to give their best for the pupils. If parents feel they have been forced to send their sons and daughters to a school they have no confidence in, they are not in a good position to back their children up in their school work and the disciplines of the school. Governors of a failing school can quickly feel powerless in the face of what they cannot influence directly, so they begin to drop out; it becomes harder and harder to have meetings that are quorate and good decisions become impossible to take.

Leadership and management of change

On their appointment, all effective new headteachers know the value of making their mark on the school as early as possible. Of the three headteachers, one was appointed to open a new Fresh Start Church school, born out of a failing community school. The two other heads had the task of getting their schools out of Special Measures. All three had the task of working within an existing structure of pupils, staff and governors, to create a new framework which would both point in new directions and also enable the people concerned to change and respond creatively to the innovations.

While they had received extra financial resources, usually tied to buildings rather than for hiring staff, the heads were in each instance the sole new factor in the school. They were challenged to produce innovative and imaginative changes which they knew would be resisted, so they required skill, a sense of timing, courage and patience to introduce the practices which would embody the new principles. In giving this leadership, the headteachers consulted widely within their schools, gaining support for their policies from governors, parents, staff and pupils although that was received neither unanimously nor immediately.

> *The drive came from me because I am the only different element (in the new situation) and I had the rock of Gospel values. I don't know whether people were motivated by my message or just not wanting to move and go. People more and more began to want to co-operate in the Church school development.* **Headteacher**

I had an interview with every member of staff, which was their time to use as they will. My mission was to bring out the good. By contrast, the HMI went through every member of staff and criticized them. I think it is for us to solve the problem, not to throw them out. We want people to do things, teach by example and love children. **Headteacher**

Two weeks ago I put out a code of Professional Behaviour, indicating where things should be brought directly to my attention. As a Fresh Start school I reckon I have to do more outside the school than is usual, and this has caused less availability. The few who left were the ones without the corporate identity. Two left and regretted it immediately. Teachers and support staff listened to my message and either made themselves a part of it or not. One, they needed to sustain their jobs and to sustain the school. The way to do it, because it was a Church school, was the values bit. No one told me how to do this. Two, it took some time on disciplinary and capability issues. I had to tell some, 'I don't like what you are doing.' Three rejected me and had to leave. In another case, someone took the support I offered them: they had never seen a model of what it could be, i.e. justice, fairness, truth in practice. Three, they needed to feel things were going right, so it was important to feed back positive messages. Church people want a school that has value; teachers do as well. Regard for Church schools is about having a more acceptable extra dimension. **Headteacher**

Jill Clough comments: One of the biggest problems with some staff who stay at and some who come to failing schools is that they can convey the impression that they are doing the head and the school a favour: the truth is that to serve children in these schools and in their home contexts is a privilege. This means that the head has to call people to account for their professional practice and be ready to deal with the open resentment which this provokes. The head can expect to be questioned by outside authorities when feathers get ruffled, but remain determined that those who are unable to recognize the privilege they have will have to go, even if this creates difficult staffing situations. To the extent that the head lives out the belief that the children in their school deserve the best, others will come to accept all that position demands, including those who may have appeared to think otherwise.

We have the staff we had, plus new staff who are the best you get. We have had difficulty appointing at all because of a shortage of available candidates. The implication in this is that old staff, for the most part, have been able to improve their performance.
Senior teacher

In having a vision and translating it so everyone became a part of it. There's clarity for everyone in the purpose: children, staff, parents. He's got compassion for people; he really cares.
Senior teacher

The Head is never angry; he treats everyone with respect, even if he doesn't agree with them. He is especially concerned about those with Special Needs or any disadvantage. He is an excellent role model to everyone in the school. He's excellent at public relations and he inspires confidence in everyone. He's got the emotional and physical stamina this place requires. He has a sense of humour and a sense of humility. Other heads I've seen are puffed up. **Deputy head**

The had doesn't say one thing and do another. People feel valued, even if they disagree with what he will do.... At the first Prize Giving the November after his arrival you could see his pride in the students and the joy in his face... He shows that he esteems them and that gives them self-esteem. The first year parents felt that here was a humble, not an overbearing person but someone with great confidence. He kept them informed.
Foundation governor

The head raised the profile of the school within the city and generated positive publicity, she changed the focus from behaviour to learning, she thought radically and gave the staff a sense of direction. **Teacher**

The head is a powerful presence within the school. She is respected by pupils and they see her as being a positive influence who has changed the school and improved their learning environment. Obviously this feeling impacts and affects the spirit of the school community. **Teacher**

The headteacher has developed a culture of strengthening the pupils' belief in their own abilities, she has expected improved teaching standards and has been able to make firm decisions if the standards are not maintained. She is well aware of the need to develop links with both local business and national groups to address an improvement in opportunities offered both to and from pupils. **Teacher**

The new frameworks on which the heads based their leadership were built on reality, what they believed could be made to happen and were neither dream nor fantasy. However, frameworks need to be implemented, at first having to rely on dispirited staff and reluctant pupils. In order to make things happen, the heads needed to have enough sensitivity to staff's feelings of weakness and sense of disappointment, as they led them. To do this they needed to identify with the staff and pupils as they were in their weaknesses, reluctance and resistances and not appear to judge or blame them. In working with the reality of the present situation, they needed to be one with the people they were working with. It called for humility and a spirit of service by the heads, so that others could respond to their Leadership.

Jill Clough comments: A spirit of service does not just happen. It develops through the head making sure that they themselves can be seen as doing some of the most difficult things in the school. This may include break duty, monitoring gates at lunch time. It also means being available, and that is more than having an 'open door' policy to one's office. From things like this the head receives respect, credibility and, in the end, their authority. This is strengthened by sharing those tasks across the staff. In addition, the head can be understood as serving the staff in how they see and provide for professional development, share out duties, reward initiative and innovation.

In all three cases, the heads saw that their new framework was a way of interpreting the vision that God had given each of them in responding to his call to be head of that particular school. The Christian model for this is the incarnation of Jesus, where he became one of us human beings, *assuming the form of a slave, bearing the human likeness, sharing the human lot.*[1*] Because of their understanding of Christ's action, the headteachers were strengthened in their own decisions and action. The model here is that of servant leadership.

Where a headteacher has a vision which they do not seek to implement through others, it may be because they appear to know the answers already and not to be close enough to the real problems and the feelings of their colleagues. However persuasive heads may be in putting forward their ideas, the staff then feel manipulated. The framework can be seen as idealistic and too risky, so any changes have to be imposed. As a result, the new structures cannot deliver what was intended unless the staff is replaced. These heads involved their staff and their pupils in the new vision for the school.

Staff's awareness of their own potential

To be associated with a failing school without doing anything effective about it becomes intolerable for any staff who can see beyond their own immediate interests. If they feel depressed, their

[*] All notes are in a separate section, on page 155.

low energy level adversely affects their own performance and they become nervous about any new challenges. The headteachers of these three schools not only organized their schools differently, but gave their staff hope and a belief that they could do justice to their profession. Thus, when staff were challenged by the new structures and educational disciplines they were able, with a few exceptions, to respond positively. Because the heads were able to keep the *whole school* in mind and yet deal with each staff member on their own level, staff found strength through their working relationships with each other and were drawn together by a new spirit of togetherness. They supported one another in tackling new things and were prepared to take risks. This new empowerment of staff was surprising even to themselves.

He had faith and belief in me as a person and in my capabilities: he did not rely on the views of others but judged me on past work. **Teacher**

I now feel empowered to do what I was trying to do before. I feel appreciated and I feel confident ... That's true of most staff. We've found avenues opened up for ourselves, we're doing things well and doing new things ... In the past whatever you did made no difference. It was very disheartening. **Senior teacher**

The head is very strong on one-to-one, sitting alongside each staff member. In a takeover you need heads to have time to sit alongside staff. From a teacher's point of view it is always the head's school, and if the head knows you and you matter this makes all the difference to what you can do. **Senior teacher**

The head could not have made the improvements alone – he needed the support of the staff, but we have done this under his direction, with his guidance. He was not afraid to get his hands dirty. He is fastidious at breathing down one's neck if he wants something done. He is tenacious. **Support staff**

Staff are valued here, there are awards for 100% attendance, there is personal interview access to the head when necessary, exceptional leave is granted where necessary, we have thoughtfully designed in service training. This also embodies the Christian ethos of each person being an individual valued by God and fellow humans. **Head of Special Educational Needs**

The staff (of this ex-local authority school) had been very wounded under so many different heads. They were 'told' they would be a Church school and they didn't know what this would mean in practice. The information about what is a Church school left a lot to be desired. They didn't know about inclusiveness and asked, 'would we be made to be Christian?' **Diocesan adviser**

The staff from the previous school were fearful they would be left behind in the re-staffing and we didn't re-apply for our jobs. The head got us training as middle managers and told us, 'I am taking you all on board. I am not asking you to be Christian.' He took us where we were. **Senior teacher, parent and governor**

Staff felt very nervous about being a Church school as to what is expected of them. **Vice chair of governors**

Before the headteacher arrived the school was in Special Measures, with very poor academic standards, poor behaviour and low levels of attendance. Staff morale was low, with many stress related illnesses. The new headteacher very soon strengthened the Senior Management Team and made great efforts to restore faith in both pupils and staff abilities. **Diocesan adviser**

Teachers in these schools responded to the way their headteachers related continually to their school, to themselves and to the pupils, as a whole. This process enabled them to overcome their own uncertainties about rising to their head's expectations and taking up their roles as staff with self-confidence, sharing encouragement as they worked together. This rise in self-esteem confirmed that, because the headteachers believed in them, the staff were able to implement the head's vision through the new school organizational framework.

Staff, whether they were Christians or not, attributed this to the Christian faith of their heads, who worked diligently with the parts, e.g. staff and pupils, learning and living, while simultaneously envisioning the whole and bringing them all alongside.

Confronted with the fluctuating morale of staff, heads could easily doubt that staff would succeed in rising to the challenge facing them. If the heads were prepared to take the risk of working with the staff as they were, that belief invited others to have a go in ways that benefited the school.

The parents believed these heads cared for their children

Though many parents were sceptical when these new heads arrived, the heads won them over by being able to express in their behaviour their care for the children. They expressed this care with such conviction that the focus and purpose of the relationship between the head and the parents became centred on the children and their learning rather than other factors.

On the basis of this shared purpose of caring for the children's learning, the heads offered to the parents a role in transforming the school community by creating partnerships of many different types with them.

> *The head sowed the seeds of the future at a meeting of 50 parents whose children were being sent to the school. There was a pre-prepared pressure group amongst them, who had the support of about two thirds of those present. Many of them had quite able children amongst them because of the demographic bulge at the time, which changed the school's ability profile. The head fielded powerful and critical questions and gave them assurance, 'I will do my utmost to ensure that your children will have a good education in this school.' Other people present at the meeting have also commented on the head's skill in handling the strong hostility that was present. Some parents said, 'A Christian will not let our children down.'* **Assistant head**

The most important thing the head does is value every child as an individual and assists each child in achieving his or her potential, whatever that may be. **Parent**

At the point where we attended induction/intake with our son, we were impressed with the way in which the head 'sold' the school to prospective parents. He upholds the Christian ethos of the school and talks with sincerity about the future direction of the school. He appears very focused on development and is in tune with his staff and pupils. **Parent**

Speaking as a parent there was always a caring ethos, but there is much more actual caring now. The way staff treat each other, and students are caring for each other. We all respect each other's space, and children are respectful to adults. **Parent governor**

Behaviour has completely changed. The children feel inspired and they value themselves. **Parent**

I was not involved with the school before and would not have sent my child to the school. However, I felt confident to do so after it became a Church school with the new head. **Parent**

He values every child; he is not interested in league tables, but the way he values the children has a knock on effect. **Parent**

Pastoral boundaries were made clear so that children, staff and parents knew how to work within them. **Assistant head**

The local community includes a large number of disinterested parents. The headteacher has worked tirelessly to encourage parental interest. The use of the sports facilities by the local community has helped and the school's reputation has improved as the head has published the success of her pupils; particularly their non-academic achievements. **Diocesan Adviser**

Asian parents prefer to go to a school that lives by values. Unless the school has values which it lives out, you miss out on parents.
Headteacher

Heads have to create conditions which enable work to be done in school with those whose parents either do not value education or find difficulty in handling their own children. The headteacher is in the best position to work with parents who are rejecting their own legal responsibilities.

Parents' confidence in the head was enhanced because they were aware that the head had values that were not simply personal. They felt that they could understand the head's Christian values, even if they did not share them. It was important that they did not feel oppressed by them. The head's values were commented on by parents, not all of whom were Christian.

The heads saw themselves as accountable to the governing body

They took governors' opinions seriously and faced them with the realities of the school. The heads, by emphasizing their responsibility to the governing body, motivated the governors to take responsibility for the school. Rather than see the governing body as a hindrance and threat to their power and control, the heads accepted their dependence on the support and feedback of the governors. They had faith and took the risk that the governors were competent to provide that support. By doing so they empowered governors.

The head believes he must always be open and clear with us. He hides nothing that worries him. Some governors feel that he is being too honest but he works on the principle that failure is acceptable but not covered up. He believes we are all working together.
Governor

When I came the majority of the governors were clergy from the local Deanery. In the view of the Diocesan adviser, this was a bad thing. They did not understand what was happening, were too busy with their own parishes and were largely inactive until Ofsted called them together in 1995, in the middle of the inspection, and told them that they were heading for being placed in Special Measures unless they took action. They were all for the Church giving up the school. A new lay chairman was found who worked hard to change the membership drawing in good people both as foundation governors and LEA governors. The present lay people are people of real Christian faith, not 'professionals' as was the case in the past. **Headteacher**

I think the old school had lost its way: we were all detached from the children, which I didn't like. Governors didn't do their job well enough. But now I think we are beginning to see change. **Governor**

By the time the head was appointed we had sorted ourselves out quite a bit. We had to face all sorts of crises: money, then buildings, then behaviour. Now he is beginning to get the curriculum together. **Governor**

The authority groups outside the school have tried to implement policy through me but I will not be moved if I feel they are trying to use power over me. Sometimes I feel like Jesus before Pilate saying that they only have authority over me to the extent that God has given it to them and when I feel that they are not using that authority I do not feel any obligation to comply with them. However, as far as governors are concerned, I do feel that they have authority with which I must work. **Headteacher**

We could see that strong measures were needed and the early retirement of the previous head was necessary. It was appropriate that governors with various new expertise were recruited. We put in place a committee procedure which I consider played an important and constructive part in the school's development, positively supporting the new head. **Vice chair**

We had a governors' meeting on the 12th of September, the day after the terrorist attacks, which brought home the importance of our work, that we recognize everyone for what they are and their contribution to the community. We are trying to give everyone the opportunity for living in a world where we have to live together.

Chair of governors

We have a problem replacing governors. It is difficult to persuade parents to stand for election to the governing body.

Chair of governors

The heads' humility, developed through their faith, has allowed them to be transparently honest with the governors about the realities of the school. This in turn has empowered the governors to *be* governors and not to opt out, or to interfere, or to degenerate into internal squabbles, but to understand that the needs of the children in their care provide the focus of their work. The chairs and the heads found ways of harnessing differences in the governing bodies constructively in the interests of the children in their different schools.

Jill Clough comments: Frankness with the governors is not just about the existing reality of the school. Heads need to inform the governors about strategies (which they approved) which have worked, and, where they have not worked, explaining why they failed. In this way, governors will really believe they are sharing the head's thinking. This may mean having to cope with painful questions from governors: after all, head and governors are all engaged with the reality of the school. By working in this way, the governors can see that they really make a difference.

School governors are men and women who volunteer to take on the responsibility, many of whom at the beginning have little or no experience of schools today. Their main preoccupations lie outside the world of education. They now have to accept responsibility for technical, financial and legal matters that are unfamiliar to them. Governors do not have a unifying profession that enables them to come together around the complexities they have to handle. Parent and teacher governors face particular challenges in that they have to position themselves very differently from their day to day position in relation to the school as they engage with other governors on the governance of the whole school. Consequently, there are many possible 'fault lines' along which these governing bodies can split. If the going gets tough again, they will have to find ways of coming together around the problem rather than being fragmented by the difficulties.

The heads recognized the part that agencies in the local community had to play if the schools were to be transformed

Transforming the schools was not just an internal exercise; the schools also had to transform their reputation in their local community by developing their relationship with the community through agencies which had influence. This was a two-way process; the more the head and the school directed positive attention to the community, the more the community directed positive attention to the head and the school. Broken ties began to be mended and new ones created. The improvement in the school's reputation in the community positively affected the internal dynamics of the school and ultimately the pupil's pride in themselves.

> *When he arrived the head embarked on a vigorous and very effective PR campaign especially in the local paper. The editor used to work for the 'Sun' so he liked negative stories about us. You could see that from the way it reported the story of our Ofsted failure. There is now a good story in almost every week.* **Deputy head**

> *The head has raised the profile of the school within the city. The local press gave positive publicity to the head's arrival which she has kept up.* **Teacher**

I adopted a high profile and went and visited influential people.
Head

We set up and led a project that linked the primary school and the two colleges of further education to provide education for people across the community. We run day time classes for the unemployed and have provided an Internet cafe on site. The effect of this has been to raise attendance at evening adult education classes in the school from 20 to 400. These are good for the community but they also generate income for the school. **Head**

We have letters and phone calls from the community congratulating the pupils on good behaviour and smart dress when they are out in the community. **Support staff**

The school's got a good reputation: you get people smiling at you when they see you're from here. We get loads of letters praising us. The school's name impresses people. We are always in the local newspaper and that helps our reputation. ... The head gets lots of praise from people who have been involved in school trips e.g. bus-drivers. **Pupil**

The choir helps to improve the reputation of the school by visiting different places. The football team always does well. Community projects such as our IT project help to project good vibes. **Pupil**

The head has put an extra screw on the propeller. He's done wonders here. He's so dedicated he is worth encouraging by this community. ... He comes to our residents' meetings and tells us what's happening. The deputy head sits on our committees and every quarter we hold a Tenants and Residents Association meeting in the school. ... There is a spirit of locality in this school.
Chair, residents association

It's a much better relationship than before. Our profile has been raised and involvement in the local community projects has increased. People are more aware of the school. **Support staff**

Recently I took some Year 7 pupils to read poems at a 'Prayers for Peace' service. This gave very good press to the school. **Teacher**

Before the head arrived the community disliked school pupils. Now the attitude to us pupils is better and I believe the community is proud of the pupils of this school ... Because we've got a new uniform the community talk to us instead of ignoring us. **Pupil**

The media has given positive press since the new head's arrival, but the reputation is still such that some parents do not wish their child to attend because they are aware that a large number of pupils come from socially deprived areas. There is still a fear that their child could be influenced by negative behaviour. **Teacher**

It does not take much for a school's fragile new reputation to be blighted – an unexpectedly poor set of results or an untoward incident involving a small number of pupils – and a climate of *'I never believed that school could really change'* can creep back into the community and anything that seems to be holding the community back is blamed on the school.

The heads, through their faith, were able to take up the role of servant to the community and thus enabled the community to take ownership of its school. The heads, in their behaviour towards the community, were saying not only that a Church school serves its community, but also that contributing to the community's welfare is part of the school's purpose.

For a church school, the local diocese is one of the most significant community bodies to which it relates.

In all three schools the appointment of new heads opened up a new relationship between the schools and their dioceses

To some extent the dioceses of these Church schools had become demotivated and had relinquished responsibility while the schools were failing. The heads not only re-established this relationship, but also brought renewed meaning to it by offering significant roles to the diocese in the transformation of the school and the development of the Church school ethos. These roles were largely carried out by the Diocesan Director of Education or the appointment of a chaplain who often had to represent the Church in the school. As these people developed their roles and relationships in the school, so the Church school ethos developed.

> *Since the head came there has been a clear commitment to Church school status. Previously the Church identity had no meaning, particularly in the local churches.* **School chaplain**

> *When it was first proposed that we become a C of E school the staff were apprehensive for themselves and for the ethnic mix of the pupils. We became a C of E school with a multi-faith intake. This is a reflection of what we should be doing in the world, not just in this town.* **Vice chair of governors**

> *When the new head arrived he came and spoke to me. He is an RC and did not know about Anglican schools. It was then I came up with the mad idea of being seconded full time to the school for a term. I wasn't there to teach RE but to be an overall Christian influence to affect everybody. I attended briefings at the beginning of each day, staff meetings, worship, looked at symbols, the school entrance area and so on. I set up links with the clergy of the four local parishes and founded a Year 7 Club. It is important that a Church school has a chaplain. It is important in a secondary school to have more than one Christian presence in the leadership because of the numbers.* **Diocesan Religious Education (RE) adviser**

Jill Clough comments: Heads all have to deal with the many outside agencies which want to tell struggling schools how to do things. It is a normal reaction to want to draw lines and keep them out, feeling that unless they are prepared to engage inside with the head and staff, they cannot be trusted. In this instance, here was someone who was willing to join with the school as an active agent, gaining authority that was much greater than that of an external 'adviser'.

This has a double value: it shows that an external agency is willing to join and be part of the internal life of the school; at the same time, it demonstrates the truth that school is connected realistically with the outside world, finding a wider sense of belonging.

My role is to ensure continuity of the Christian ethos, to establish patterns with Cathedral Services and work with local priests, to see that all departments relate to faith development and be explicit about this. **Chaplain**

Having the diocese alongside is important for every Church school but especially so for a new one. That was what I could do.
Diocesan RE adviser

I sometimes have to remind the head we are in a Church of England school, it is an Anglican foundation. Living that foundation out means Christianity has a more predominant place.
Diocesan RE Adviser

The central point is the importance of working out theologically what education is for and how that is translated into practice. It needs to be personal at its core but it is also about the whole. This is true of all our successful Voluntary Aided schools. The foundation governors need to be in the majority and need to be active not passive in their faith. The Diocesan Director of Education has the right to give advice alongside the LEA and their advice needs to be Christian in its essence. **Diocesan Director of Education**

The position of school chaplain has had the effect of adding an extra dimension to the lives of our students and also of our staff. I feel that there is greater concern for care and consideration towards others. This position also gives our students a chance to consider their own feelings and beliefs. This, in my experience, does not happen to such a degree in a non-denominational school. With the chaplain on the school site the students gradually adopt a more relaxed and open dialogue about religion and social issues. There does not seem to be any anti-feeling about religion, in fact the students are quite aware of the importance of the Church and act accordingly, this builds strength in our students, a form of self-discipline. **Deputy head**

Jill Clough comments: In a church school, the head has available, in the diocese, a potentially massive resource. This is not simply a bureaucratic resource – in the best sense of the word – because the Church of England, being the established church, is constitutionally committed to serve the whole population whoever they may be. Where a school that has been failing or has been marginalized, it makes a great deal of difference when a 'non-educational' body takes a particular interest in the school's recovery, embracing the school and joining it in the struggle to recover. In this way, students are offered the opportunity to think of their school as potentially healthy and credible in the local context. This happens most effectively when the external agency is not seen as having an external agenda – be it political, commercial, or other agenda. In this case, children and young people know they are not being exploited in someone else's battle, so they can feel that they are seen as valuable in their own right. Of course, if the diocese is seen as being interested simply in recruiting 'pew fodder', its agency is little different from being part of a commercial or political purpose. The way the head handles the relationship is critical in giving the relationship a positive shape.

Though I had been a head of RC schools in the private sector I had no experience of working within the Church of England's state school structure. I was greatly helped by the chair of governors who knows the Church of England hierarchy and also by the LEA's Director of Education, even though he is an atheist. **Head**

There is a difference in the backing the school gets from the Church because he is a Christian. He's changed the attitude of the local Deanery Synod who used to be opposed to the school, indeed they tried to get rid of it. They recently gave a grant to us of £5,000 towards our getting Specialist School status.

School business manager

All three heads either created new supportive structures for themselves or were helped to do so by the diocese. In all three cases, they had the intention of being *inclusive schools*, open to serving their local communities as they are. The heads themselves, though none of them was an Anglican, all led from the front, setting out to change the local church policies where necessary. Underlying their intention to lead schools that were open to all those with religious faith and with none, was a clear conviction that Christ came primarily not to make human beings Christian, but that they might have life more fully as human beings. They saw that a Church of England school, as part of the structure of the established Church, is committed to serve the whole population.

This places a Church of England school in a different position from other schools founded on a faith basis: Roman Catholic, Jewish, Muslim or other schools may adopt a feeling of responsibility for the whole of the local community, but there is no obligation on them to do that. They are set up to serve their own people. Anglican schools may baulk at the position they hold and seek to function in sectarian ways, attracting much negative publicity as a result. This was not the case with the three schools we studied nor with many, many others who attract little attention to what they really do, but face much criticism which ricochets at them from the other few.

As these schools gained reputations as being successful in doing good work for their pupils, they came under pressure to be selective in their intake. This was considerable in one place where another community school had been built to serve the estate alongside them. The conviction of the heads and their governors that they lead inclusive schools was tested and as their reputations rise the testing becomes greater. The challenge for their successors will be to sustain the schools as inclusive.

Jill Clough comments: Heads of unpopular schools come under pressure, especially, but not solely, from governors, to become oversubscribed. If the school is oversubscribed, the impression can be given that the school is selecting its intake on some (covert) criteria that preserve its popularity (and effectiveness) in order to handle the excess numbers. This can have the satisfying effect of playing to parents' ambitions for their children because they want the best for them. To be a truly inclusive school, heads need to build sound working relations with their local communities which dispel the myth of selection while underlining the service to the community as a whole.

The result of enabling people to belong

Signs and symbols of success

Headteachers appointed to 'failing' schools are expected to include targets which act as signals of their school's success. We have drawn on these in our earlier descriptions of the schools' achievements: better test and exam results, better attendance figures, lower exclusion rates. These are not in themselves any more than surface symptoms of deeper and more important things happening. It is these deeper things, less tangible and harder to describe, which are actually much more the true signs of health in a school, signs to which these heads attended. We found two parallel interacting strategies apparent in all three schools.

The first was to provide pupils with the knowledge and skills relevant to their success in a given curriculum. This came through offering them the incentive of good teaching. Pupils/students could then learn with greater freedom, attaining objectively set standards which were appropriate to their stage of educational development. The second strategy was to enrich pupils as human beings, as they proceed towards becoming mature adults. This was done through their acquiring values which could equip them to work with others in contributing to the well-being of something larger than their individual selves. This began with the school and moved on to understanding themselves as part of the wider society.

The three headteachers were not only decisive in declaring these strategies, but they were prepared to face the challenge of working with and through their staff and also, to different degrees, in consultation with their pupils. To achieve results, all three began by accepting the resources which their Church schools were offering. They developed in pupils and staff a sense of identity, in particular, a sense of corporate identity which grew from their feeling of belonging to the school. They saw the *outwardness* of identity which is signified by pupils being in uniform, which enabled children to see their role as members together of their school, which is different from simply being individuals.

We will say more about this dimension later, but will open up the question here. The *inwardness* of identity was developed by transforming school assemblies into worship services. Each school used different symbols to further this process. One school reversed the normal placing of the chairs in the hall so that they faced a previously ignored triptych, drawn by a nationally famous artist, which depicts the Trinity. Another school, which already had the asset of a church immediately adjoining the school, brought an Anglican priest onto the staff to be head of Religious Education and to lead the worship as chaplain. The third school, with its large Muslim membership, re-organized the back of the stage in the main hall as an Inter-faith Centre with Christian symbols exhibited at times of worship.

In the worship, headteachers and other members of staff spoke briefly on themes and, in some schools, led the prayers. Worship was never seen as the vehicle for notices and general information-giving sessions.

Jill Clough comments: Every coming together of the school as a whole – or of as much of it as accommodation will allow – is of great psychological significance to the sense of school as community. All such occasions, whether for assembly, celebration or worship, demand the same level of attention and preparation. If a head wishes to change the values and ethos of their school they need to devote as much time to planning and preparation of assembly as they do to Prize Day. It is also important that the students recognize that such preparation has taken place without their feeling that someone is making a meal out of their hard work and expects some gratitude.

Corporateness included staff in that prayers were introduced to early morning staff meetings, the themes of which were then carried on in tutor groups. In one school, new staff were inducted by the whole school joining in prayers for them in the church, followed by the chaplain handing them a lighted candle. After that, the headboy and headgirl greeted them as new members of the school.

Gradually blossoming corporateness like this had an impact upon pupils' behaviour towards others. They also paid more attention to their class lessons and learning. Because their starting point was low both academically and socially, progress was slow though sure. One school had more difficulties than the others: though they had not reached their GCSE targets at the time of the study, Ofsted were satisfied with their overall achievement. The other two schools had exceeded their targets and received praise for their achievements.

Our attendance has increased and we have help and support with our studies. The head also helps us realize about our future. **Pupil**

The pupils haven't 'succeeded' yet, but there is a move in the right direction ... enabling people to feel safe, no longer out of control. There is a peer support system ... improved bullying and changed the culture ... we've moved from being a victim school. **Teacher**

There has been no improvement in A-C examination results though we have a higher percentage taking exams ... There is a question whether teachers still know what a good grade C looks like. Homework has been tightened up, though parents did not think it mattered whether their children came to school or not. Children are still kept at home on the slightest excuse, our attendance is about 80%, we need 90%. **Chair of governors**

Exam results are still poor but the parent meeting attendance has improved from 30% to over 50%. **Governor**

I didn't think we were a failing school ... the school was not as bad as it was painted. The new head put initiatives into moving forward; our exam results are slowly improving but they have taken five years to achieve. **Support staff**

Recently I find the school has entered a more challenging period where pupils' progress is slowing and there is a tendency to feel that things are not moving forward, which can lead to some disillusionment. **Teacher**

All good heads face the challenge of performance and character and find their own way of overcoming the limitations of their schools. The test is whether the changes are solely due to their personal skills, professional confidence and the strength of their personality, or whether the principles they bring to the school can percolate through the staff, pupils, governors and school community. If it is the latter, everyone can not only experience the fruit of the change, but also take ownership of it. As a result, the changes will continue after the head has left. Christian heads are in the same situation.

The single-mindedness of these headteachers indicated their passion about the Christian foundation which their Church schools provided both for education and human development. They believed in transformation, but knew it called for more than they themselves could do: it would result from the work and grace of God. As a self-defined atheist, the Chief Education

Officer of the LEA asked one new Christian head on appointment, whom he had found through a headhunter, 'If you are successful how much would you attribute to yourself or to the Almighty?' Her reply was, 'God can get all the credit.' All three heads had the same humility, but then they all knew it was up to them to make it happen.

The school becomes a place to be proud of

Members of the school and those associated with it felt good about it. They related to it consciously as a 'good object', and handled themselves in ways which reflected that good feeling. This expressed *self-discipline* rather than codes of behaviour which had been imposed. The wearing of uniform and wearing it appropriately was not a problem. Events like prize-giving were joyful occasions. Parents were glad that their children attended their school. New buildings reflecting investment in the school made a significant contribution to people feeling pride in the school. These investments were signs that others in significant places believed the school was worth investing in, and valued the work going on.

> **Jill Clough comments:** People with low status feel themselves to be of little worth in the eyes of others. So, in turning a school round, almost anything that gives a visible sign of high status should be procured in service of the task of transformation. At the very least, a new design of the school letter head or a new uniform provide tangible signals, while new buildings (so long as they are intelligently designed) shout out the message fortissimo. The head needs to brace himself for accusations of 'squandering resources on minutiae' from the old guard!

It has a good reputation, you get people smiling at you when they see you're at [our school]. We get loads of letters praising us ... The school name impresses people. We are always in the local paper and that helps our reputation. **Pupil**

We have letters and phone calls from the community congratulating the pupils on good behaviour and smart dress in the community. **Support staff**

The media has given us a positive press since the new head's arrival. **Teacher**

I am glad to send my children to this school because they treat you with respect there. **Sikh parent**

The pupils are beginning to feel it is a place to be proud of. They get no back up from home, parents themselves had a poor education. **Teacher**

Since the head came, everywhere you look things have changed; buildings don't have graffiti and they looked cared for; the new buildings left some people aghast and they said, 'too good for us'; but people are now beginning to take a pride in the school, both pupils and staff. **Governor**

The children have a growing sense of loyalty to the school. For example, there was a boy who always wore a red shirt, but when the HMI visited he took the trouble to change his shirt and to wear uniform. **Senior manager**

Because we've got a new uniform the community talk to us instead of ignoring us. **Pupil**

It is said that pride comes before a fall; but that is a reminder that one's sense of belonging to something worthwhile needs to be rooted in reality. If the pride is based on a fantasy of the school, being blind to or denying its failings, then the situation is dangerous. If the head had misled teachers, pupils and parents (and indeed others, including inspectors) about the quality of the school because it shamed them, it would have made the next head's task of transforming the school immeasurably harder because pointing to faults had only previously been seen as unacceptable behaviour instead of an incentive to improve. Being proud is no justification for lying.

The three heads demonstrated in their own lives the capacity to be openly identified with the Christian Church, though realizing its weaknesses and failings without being ashamed of it, and believing that despite these deficiencies God continues to use the Church to extend his love to all people. They were strengthened by God to accept the realities of their school's shortcomings, believing it was worth investing their lives in changing the situation. For them, the school despite 'failing' was a 'good' school from the beginning. It was their leadership which raised morale so that in turn governors, pupils and parents could take a proper pride in their school and feel good about it.

BEING the head

Just because one has been appointed to a position does not mean that a person *is* the head. A school only has a head once the person begins to 'fill' the position, to give it flesh and bones, to convey and to provoke feelings – both positive and negative. We will say more about this in Chapter 3 (Principles of Leadership) but, for the moment, the point we are making is that these three headteachers worked 'in role' and this was evident to everyone else in their school, and enabled them to take up their roles as pupils, teachers and others.

These effective headteachers were able to work consistently for the benefit of the school

As we have shown, they were clear that their primary focus was on the pupils and their learning to develop as potential adults. Management and leadership skills ensured that their staffs and other resources were also directed to that end, despite the disruptions, emergencies, mistakes and obstacles they had to deal with in the day to day life of the school.

Our three headteachers were able to do this in their different local communities:

He does things to benefit the school as a whole and not just for individual people. **Pupil**

He has created an atmosphere of confidence and sense of direction, everyone is excited about the future development of the school. His positive and hardworking attitude has passed on to the children. **Support staff**

There has been a great effect on the spirit of the school community due to the head's leadership by knowing what he wants to happen and having the confidence to make it happen. **Governor**

What I needed to do was to create an environment within which good teaching could take place. So it was the immediate practical things that I did which I felt were key. **Headteacher**

Jill Clough comments: Heads bringing about transformation in a schools find themselves balancing the overtly 'value laden' with the 'practical'. Here attention to the detail of seeing things from the pupils' perspective is critical: Where will a child's locker be in relation to their general movement around the school? How will access to different rooms be most easily arranged? What does it feel like to be queuing for lunch? Can the service counters be extended to speed things up? And so on.

We try to create young people who have a mind-set about themselves and the institution so that they can become learners. If you've got pupils who feel positive about themselves and about learning, they can go to class to be partners with the teachers. **Headteacher**

The headteacher has developed a culture of strengthening the pupils' belief in their own abilities and has expected improved teaching standards and been able to make firm decisions if the

standards are not maintained. She is well aware of the need to develop links with both local business and national groups to address an improvement in opportunities offered both to and from pupils.
Teacher

Before the current head came there was no sense of vision in the school but she has a vision which is bigger than the school, seen by the way she speaks of her desire to enable our children to succeed, it is more important to her than her career. She believes that loving the children is the way she can help them to succeed.
Diocesan Adviser

Yes, I do think that students make an effort because of the head. He motivates us during assemblies and gives us an insight on what he is intending to do.
Pupil

The most important thing the head has done is to take charge, he has begun and still is rewarding students for hard work. **Pupil**

It is the nature of the way the head has understood and articulated his understanding of the vision and his role which has made the difference. His pattern has been picked up by the governors. This is why values are so important; the head says that values are the basis for everything.
Deputy Head

The head's motivation is us! He cares about us, about trying to improve things and he provides new facilities. He asks our opinions.
Pupil

There is a quality of intensity in the way the heads concentrated on their task. They were not only doing the right things, they were able to get things right in the eyes of others – pupils, staff, parents and governors. The school's transformation was the result of the spirit of willing co-operation, although the extent of the transformation varied because of the schools' starting positions, and the length of time the heads had been in post. As we will show, the motivation for this love and direction came from their Christian faith.

There are levels of effectiveness among headteachers and all of them made mistakes. Their effectiveness depended on how they dealt with their mistakes – owning up to them, denying them, keeping them private or, when appropriate, dealing with them in public.

The Christian faith of the headteachers

This project was instigated to examine the transformative effect of Christian headteachers. The three heads of the selected schools saw their Christian faith as something they experienced personally and which they expressed publicly and shared with the whole school through its worship. For them, their faith was a vital factor in the educational process of their school which, being a Church school, gave them the space to live out their beliefs through every aspect of its life.

> *Although not all of our students come from Christian families, they know that the head is a committed Christian and respect him for that too. The head leads by example in the way he deals with people.* **Teacher**

> *The Head has a belief in his calling and vocation, and in the guidance of the Holy Spirit ... He professes his faith in an interesting and in no sense formidable way.* **Governor**

> *He has strong beliefs and tries to reflect them in the way he runs the school.* **Pupil**

> *I have faced all sorts of difficulties and when I find myself at the end of my tether, I pray 'God, you called me here, what are you going to do about this situation?' God has never let me down. An early prayer was that if God had called me to close the school down that I should be able to do that with dignity. I now know that it was not for closure that I came, but for a task which has not yet ended.* **Headteacher**

When I met the Chief Education Officer we had a set to, no one had ever challenged me like this by asking how much would you attribute to yourself or to the Almighty. I replied, 'God can get the credit.' **Headteacher**

The impact on the staff (of the head) is enormous. Everything is exact and the head encourages but she also loves the pupils by using a stick. Her Christian conviction is quite instinctive: it comes from her cultural background. She creates a general ethos around her which is accepted by everybody in the school. **Teacher**

If something critical happens, the head says, 'We will go to Church today to pray about it.' **Senior manager**

The head put Gospel values at the heart of the school, he makes frequent reference to these values when talking to staff and pupils. **Teacher**

He does not force Christianity upon pupils but encourages them to respect each other's beliefs. **Teacher**

His openness to ecumenical and inter-faith relationships was important for this school. He has stuck with a resolution born of his own beliefs. **Foundation director**

He came across at interview with passion. His Christian leadership from the start, he didn't boot out staff. He has handled it in a gentle, positive way. **Governor**

He sees himself as having a mission for the school and that's why God sent him here. He believes that God will help him to achieve that mission and help to turn the school around ... I'm not a church-goer myself. **Assistant Head**

These extracts focused on the personal behaviour of the heads as they were experienced by pupils, staff and others. They show the strength of their faith in working with others most of whom did not claim to be Christian and sometimes were members of other faiths. In no instance has evidence been offered by anyone indicating any objection to a head's way of expressing their faith.

Criticism has been directed at Church schools because some people perceive that they give a one-sided view of religion. Critics suggest that religion is a private matter and needs to be bracketed out; some say that it is only a matter of life-style; others say that Christianity should become only one religion among many in religious studies. Such an approach maintains that in school, religion is to be treated intellectually and not to be fostered as personal belief.

The Heads' experience and practice as non-Anglicans

The project did not investigate the personal religious beliefs of the headteachers. It concentrated on what the heads said about the way they offered their leadership and how staff, pupils, parents and governors commented on how heads *'behaved their faith'* as spelled out in previous sections of this chapter. They had in common, decisiveness and readiness to take risks about the Christian dimension of their leadership. They were transparent in leading staff prayers in morning staff meetings and in the provision of Christian worship for the school as a whole. Nevertheless, they were prepared to live with the uncertainty of their decisions, just like Abraham who, by faith in God left his home to go into strange territory *'not knowing where he was going'*. [Hebrews 11:8]

Two of the three heads were practising Roman Catholics, and the third head was a Free Church Evangelical, but he had left a deputy headship in a Roman Catholic school to take up his present post. That all three could lead the transforming process of Anglican Church schools while strongly retaining their own denominational allegiances, demonstrated the inclusiveness of their own beliefs in working in the ethos of another denomination.

Their own presence as head is a proclamation of inclusiveness, which they saw not as compromise, but as a wider vision to be extended to all. They conceived their own experience as allowing God to use them *for the benefit of the whole community*, based on a Church of England school and not primarily for the benefit of the Church itself. It seems right to assume that their Roman Catholic experience had developed in them a sense of professionalism, a discipline of consistency and concern for pupils. Through their lack of knowledge of the Church of England practices, they lacked the full freedom to engage with community leaders in order to service them. Nevertheless, this was not in the end a disadvantage. As one head put it:

> *I do experience a tension in coming from a Roman Catholic background to the Church of England, but the benefit is that it has led me to develop my faith more than I could do in a Catholic school.*

Each head had asked for expert guidance from Church of England officers and clergy about how to work within the Church of England ethos and culture. In one, the head had successfully recruited an Anglican priest as head of RE and as chaplain; since then he has been appointed assistant head. In one school, the head accepted the offer of a Diocesan schools adviser for a term to teach and to manage the worship process. In another, the Bishop had appointed a part-time chaplain to help, but he had not been able to offer sufficient appropriate support, so the Bishop had to look for another priest/chaplain. All three heads ensured that religious education was well taught. However, we had no evidence about the impact of RE, positive or negative, on the pupils, whereas there was plenty of evidence offered about worship.

Jill Clough comments: An experienced headteacher advises that if one really wants faith to be alive on one's school one should not muddle worship and religious education.

Religious education needs to be taught with the same rigour and objectivity as mathematics or languages. In worship, the experience is different and the learning, because learning has a place in worship, is different. Pupils will experience different values (not ones which conflict with those experienced in lessons) which are communicated centrally through behaviour. For example, 'boredom' during an act of worship has a different meaning from 'boredom' in a lesson: as indicated by the pupil's quotation about not wanting to listen because 'they go on about bad things and you don't want to get depressed'. Preaching in an act of worship is part of the plan and how it happens is properly integrated into the overall design, while preaching in a lesson is out of place. Children have spiritual insights which can be brought to the surface and released in worship, as indicated in the comment about the destruction of the Twin Towers on 11 September 2001, but such feelings have only a small place in a lesson, unless this is negotiated with the pupils, in which case it can be extraordinarily powerful. Most children intuitively know the difference between the two situations. As the headteacher making this comment said, ensuring this difference is part of the work of the head.

The centrality of worship in these schools

Ofsted report after Ofsted report includes the comment that governors are breaking the law because of the failure of schools to conduct a 'daily act of worship which has a broadly Christian character'. As Church of England schools, it was unlikely that they would break the law in that way. However, all three took the *'act of worship'* extremely seriously, though accommodation prevented them gathering the whole school together in a single place. A factor here was that their practices would be inspected under Section 23 by Anglican inspectors.

Worship as a key school activity

Each of the three headteachers tackled the issue of worship differently owing to circumstances, but they were all convinced that it was central to their school's life. Two heads replaced 'school assemblies' with worship, making other provision for communication of school announcements. They reordered the halls in which they met in order to provide Christian symbols to facilitate the worship. The third school had the parish church adjacent to the school so they assembled there under the ministry of the school chaplain. Each school had daily briefing staff meetings with prayers and some with 'thoughts for the day'.

Having worship every day starts the day for both staff and pupils in a Christian frame of mind. It refocuses them. **Support staff**

Worship and assembly are crucial. They are informative, educational and they invite reflection. Children take on board the message, and they talk about it afterwards. He praises the children. **Teacher**

The Head has a balanced approach to worship, he gives room for the individual to choose, he respects the individual. **Governor**

The assemblies and worship sessions create a positive atmosphere in the school. The head often played a piece of music to emphasize the point he was trying to get across. I particularly remember an assembly where he played 'Chains' by Tina Turner. If my memory serves me correctly he was talking about emotional/spiritual freedom. That assembly must have been taken about three years ago, however it has stayed with me since. **Ex-pupil**

There is no discernible impact on students' attitudes from worship; it's more the attitude of staff and their role-modelling which makes the difference. **Teacher**

For those who believe in God, assemblies and worship are a good influence but for the rest, they just want to get out quickly.
Support staff

A lot of the time you don't want to listen because they're about the bad things that are going on and you don't want to get depressed.
Pupil

We have a whole school assembly in the local church, Lower School on Thursday and Upper School on Wednesday, for 20 minutes. I used to give the reflection, but now it is done by the chaplain. I greet the children and always find something to praise them about. So far there are no hymns or songs. **Headteacher**

The staff and pupils accepted that it was a Church school, but the pupils have very limited perspectives, so the head was advised by the churches to take a softly softly approach. People come to me regularly about personal relations, two or three are boys.
Chaplain

He hasn't gone overboard on Christian worship but has developed from a values base. A significant initiative has been the Faith Development Centre, which has got good support from all faiths. I have wanted to go further, i.e. eucharists for staff, I would like it calendared in monthly. **Governor**

Values were key, and liturgy for the start of every day. As staff became involved one read a prayer about needing other people. Educational excellence is about 'decent people and values'. You have to go from Values to Process, the school is about partnership with parents, dealing with children, Gospel values and so on.
Headteacher

I said it was about behaviour in a Christian manner that was supportive of our Church school ethos. They could all do that because of the values I was expecting the school to uphold. I talked to them about Christ's values at the heart and the way He taught them. I said I was more interested in the Christian faith than the church adherence! **Headteacher**

In worship, special attention was paid to everyone's position, though each school was different. One school's Faith Development Centre had symbols of all faiths, where the Christian symbols were displayed during the whole school worship; another reversed the seating of chairs in front of a Christian triptych, while the third met in the parish church, making other arrangements for other faiths where requested.

In all three, headteachers greeted pupils as they entered, usually in tutor groups, to give value to individuals. Leading worship was shared with senior management, staff, pupils and visitors. The purpose was to encourage everyone to share in the spirit of worship and to show that God is at the centre of life, and in particular at the centre of this school's life. While some pupils said they found it boring and a waste of time, there were occasions when everyone present was caught up together, for example, in one school where the three new staff were presented with lighted candles on their welcome by staff and students. It was also the case that the same students commented favourably on the headteachers' Christian faith, which was most frequently evident to them in worship.

Jill Clough comments: Many heads will speak about their having a battle with staff about how to behave in assembly and worship. Staff are there as worshippers themselves and need to behave like that: this calls for them to be silent, not to become preoccupied with 'discipline', fussing about how students are dressed (this needs to be sorted before the meeting); those who are outside the hall (and ideally all staff should seek to attend if at all possible; worship is not 'the head's event') should take account of what is happening inside the hall, behaving in ways that do not disrupt what is going on. The Senior Leadership Team (or whatever it is called) may have to work to 'train' students and staff how to come together as a totality, perhaps suggesting some form of preparation (say a minute's silence in tutor groups before coming to the hall). Communities need to learn how to come together collectively, without feeling that the only reason they are being assembled is to experience the power of whoever conducts the worship or assembly. If this coming together is done well, the move onwards to taking other roles in the school's daily life can be made easier because one has a sense of the whole.

Above all, the time for worship encouraged pupils to experience what it is to belong to something bigger than themselves and to look outwards to others. To love God meant loving everyone of whatever faith. However, in times of reflection, we all discover resistances in ourselves to change and some negativity is to be expected. Only where there is consistency and reliability in the school will worship provide the space for staff and pupils to discover the truth in themselves. The openness pupils had in giving their different reactions to us was evidence of their freedom to be themselves. Worship contributed to that freedom by showing how pupils could widen their vision and raise their behaviour to take responsibility and make positive relations by forgiving and asking forgiveness of others. Some of them also appreciated that Christ was a source of help and strength in doing this.

Much criticism of Church schools is directed to the injustice of imposing religious ideas upon pupils who do not have the freedom to think for themselves. This raises a question about education. Do not pupils require to learn discipline in order to take authority for themselves? School worship is a form of discipline which provides a quality of life which is not available through other aspects of the normal curriculum. Whereas mathematics, science and the humanities provide growth in intellectual intelligence, and the arts, media and sporting activities contribute to the development of emotional intelligence, is it possible that worship can foster moral, spiritual and social qualities which, alongside the other subjects, lead to the *development of the whole person* in the context of society? All subjects, combined with effective worship, can foster the imagination as pupils journey into the unknown adult world.

Opening minds and hearts through worship

Worship in Church schools is frequently discounted by outsiders because of confusion with sectarianism in so-called 'faith' schools. It may appear paradoxical, but these three Christian heads were more 'open' *because* of their faith. Their faith caused them to value the pupils as whole persons above their own career interests. Sensitivity to this factor led heads to use worship as a means of extending pupils' thoughts and feelings outwards towards others rather than to focus down on private needs. Pupils and staff could therefore experience themselves as belonging to the whole school, transcending their experience as individuals, while not inhibiting it.

The approach to worship in these schools responded to the need to integrate worship into the cultural norms which are the heritage of British society. They did this in a manner which opened society, with its Christian heritage, to people of other faiths. Ultimately it is the actual outcomes of Church schools, expressed through their graduates, which will enable questions about Britain as a truly inclusive society to be considered.

Brief thoughts for the day were presented at worship variously by staff, the head, the chaplain and pupils to facilitate this process of participation by all. Such worship exemplified *inclusion while recognizing diversity of ability*, race, age, culture and where relevant, religion. The spirit of worship was carried throughout the schools by tutor group meetings and course/year meetings, backed up by briefings and a 'thought for the day' at the daily staff meetings.

> *This had to be a Christian school where all faiths were acceptable. The question for me is on whose behalf are heads acting? Church schools are on behalf of the Church for the world, not on behalf of heads. My principle is, get the theology right. In a multicultural setting we must be a servant for the whole people and be sure enough of our basis to be a church for the whole community. We have to be secure enough to make room for other faiths otherwise you are getting into a bigoted system. You have to take risks.*
> **Governor**

I'm a person in this school and other people need to be persons too. As the head I am not just Polyfilla, filling in all the gaps. I am leading people with what people call traditional Christian moral values but I don't demand that they be Christians themselves. This gives them values about citizenship which are more important than the values they see in the pop idols. **Headteacher**

The most effective assembly I have witnessed since arriving at the school was the morning after September 11th. The pupils demonstrated a real sense of understanding of the situation, sorrow, and a sense of belonging as a group. **Teacher**

My son claims that stories told in assemblies have morals and teach pupils that it is never too late to change: putting bad experiences behind you and striving to become a better person. **Parent**

The Headteacher hasn't gone overboard on Christian worship but has developed from a values base. A significant initiative has been the Inter-Faith Development Centre, which has got good support from all faiths. **Governor**

He relates assemblies to the real world and raises self esteem. **Parent**

He led Thought for the Day every day in the staff-room before we went out. Gradually people began to offer to do it instead, and then to take it into registration. It's very helpful to go out with a thought in your head. He gave topics for assemblies, and a calendar of relevant Christian thoughts, plus things for other religions. **Teacher**

I remember an assembly about imaginary trees and stuff because it was so bizarre. The moral was that you shouldn't take things for granted because one day they might be gone. It made me think I shouldn't take things for granted and made me appreciate things more and be nicer to people. **Pupil**

Morning briefings – they started secular and became more Christian as time passed. **Diocesan adviser**

Key was my first assembly where I presented universal values of love, joy, peace, honesty and particularly forgiveness – everyone could sign up to these. My purpose was to work from values to belief, which happened gradually. **Headteacher**

I believe the assemblies allow the school to reflect on everyday life and how we can work to make it better. **Pupil**

Assemblies help us see another way of thinking. Awards are given out with lots of encouragement, we are told stories and examples of things, like forgiving people. We have visitors come in to talk to us about faith or a special occasion. They help by teaching us more about Christianity while not pushing us into anything. **Pupil**

Despite the slight confusion in what that last pupil said, the three heads were meticulous in distinguishing the use of assemblies for worship from other school assemblies, finding other avenues for communicating necessary information to the rest of the school. For them, worship set the tone of the school and involved the risk that if they failed in creating a calm environment for worship then the whole Church school framework would eventually collapse or become meaningless.

Worship stimulates multi-directional relationships. Pupils will only become aware of them gradually and spasmodically as they find ways to express their feelings and thoughts and learn to act appropriately instead of opting out through boredom.

The goodness and love of God will become real for pupils if the senior staff, and especially the head, become good models in their school relationships. Their open relationship with God causes pupils to see the value of true relations with each other. This evolving process will be blocked if pupils (and staff) are anxious about their identity. Being ready to lose one's identity (life) for Jesus' sake opens the way to realize one's humanity more fully. Worship provides an opportunity for this inner work, which was deepened when pupils and staff chose to celebrate the Holy Communion held periodically in the three schools. Taking things seriously does not mean being always serious in worship; people need to be engaged, to be stimulated by hope and joy (fun), with unexpected moments of awe.

Where everything is predictable and leaders carry on routinely without conviction, everyone becomes bored, there is nothing stimulating to engage with. Because of the quality of faith necessary for leadership of worship, headteachers even though convinced Christians, may not always rise to the occasion, if their level of professional competence and management does not establish the corporate discipline required. Where this occurs, the value of being a Church school and being a place worth belonging to runs the risk of being lost.

Chapter 3

Underlying Principles of Leadership

In the next three sections we will explore principles of leadership in three specific areas that were significant for these headteachers. We will explore how they led persons – children and young people and adults. To do this we will introduce concepts about human behaviour in organizations and explore how those relate to transforming schools; we will go on to describe a particular way of thinking about role, the roles of pupil and teacher, and how these can be thought about creatively in schools; and from that we will show how important it is for heads and teachers to understand about power and authority if schools are to function in the best interests of children.

Next, in exploring principles of the leadership of systems, we will explore the central importance of working with one's lived experience. To do that calls for an understanding of human systems of activity (which need to be thought about in a different way from other, mechanistic, systems) which leads us on to describe the way a headteacher's behaviour is the keystone of leadership in transforming a school.

Thirdly, we open up the significance of worship in these three church schools as the activity where the most significant emotional and intellectual work of transformation can take place. This enables us to explore the function of corporate acts such as assembly in the life of any school, and the place of 'religion' in all schools.

3.1 Leadership of person

The background to our understanding

We came to these three schools with experience and ideas about the processes by which children grow up and become adults, and about how schools contribute to that. Those of us on the project have worked with children, been teachers, have worked with heads and their staffs, been school governors, have researched and consulted to organizations of many different kinds and have brought up children. The ideas developed from those experiences have been tested by our work on this study and they have been developed further as a result.

This section describes the concepts, models and principles which we used, expressing them here as we now understand them, applied to these schools that have transformed.

A working model of human interaction and social development

Children inevitably become adults. So all societies have evolved ways of enabling their children to grow up and to be equipped to take over the running of that society from their elders. Rituals and procedures have been used to enable knowledge, skills, beliefs, values and visions of the future to be communicated from generation to generation. This is true whether we think of historic societies such as tribes in South American tropical rain forests, Pacific Islands, hill tribes in the Himalayas or nomads in Arabian deserts. Each culture evolves its own rituals and procedures.

In our 'civilized' societies we carry out the same processes in our own ways. What is different for us today is that, where earlier societies tended to do most of what needed to be done in the context of the family, the village and the tribe, we have 'invented' institutions called 'schools' to which every child is expected to go. These are not the same institutions as those used by distinguished Greeks and Romans to bring up their children in their cities, nor are they the same as those bodies created in England to supply cathedrals and churches with those who could sing the liturgy (choir schools) and understand the language of the Bible (grammar schools).

The provision of universal schooling since the late 19th century raises new obstacles to what needs to be done if our children are to be fully equipped to join us in mutual responsibility for the kind of society we live in, preparing them to inherit it from us in due course and who will then be responsible for it in their own way. Too often there are obstacles which we seem to have ignored or whose significance we have underestimated. There is that well-known and oft-quoted African saying: *It takes a whole village to bring up a child.*

Of course, universal schooling is necessary, given how complicated is the state of our knowledge and the levels of skill needed to function today; but creating a schooling for everybody has made some other things – fundamental things – harder to do.

What was evident to us in the study of church schools was that all three heads we worked with, for whatever reason, probably sound instincts combined with good previous professional experience, worked in ways that expressed the natural processes which foster growing up to full adulthood. So we felt that the model of processes of human interaction and social development which we had developed over thirty years, actually provides a way to understand the reality of interactions, especially between children and adults.

The model helps us to visualize the natural growth of an individual from childhood to becoming someone who can function in society. We think that, like 'white' light and the colours of the spectrum, the interactions that lead to overall growth of persons can be refracted into four different processes. Earliest

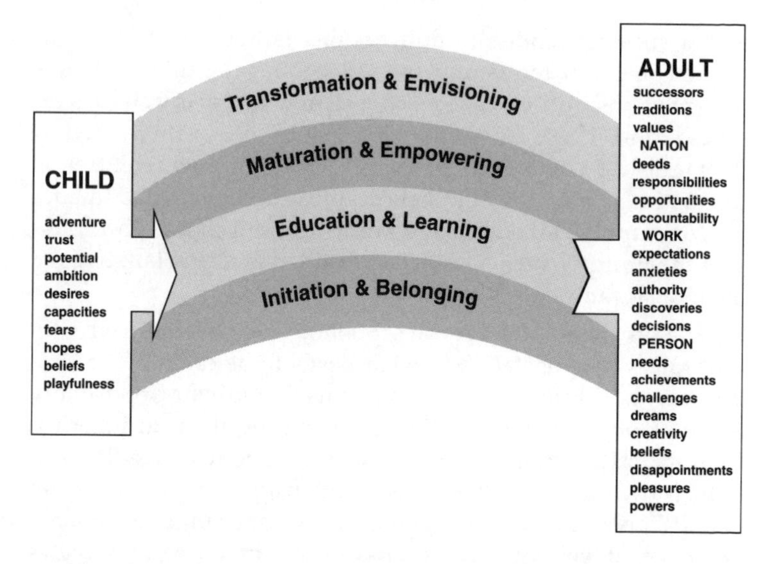

Figure 1: The Reed Rainbow of human interaction and social development. (See Frontispiece for a larger version, in colour.)

societies handled these in their own ways and we can now seek to foster them in ours. The model describes what *actually takes place naturally*, influenced to a greater or lesser degree every time any child meets any adult, not because anything is planned, but because this is how we are made as human beings. It provides a practical frame whereby actual experience of real encounters between children and adults can be explored, understood, priorities worked out and new initiatives taken in the light of analysis and thought.

The Reed Rainbow (Diagram 1) is based on the reality that a child, if he or she continues to live, will grow into an adult.[2] The question is, what kind of adult? The family is the natural habitat for initial stages of growth, followed generally in societies by introduction into working life (often accompanied by initiation ceremonies, led by experienced adults, which involve learning values, attitudes, skills and physical disciplines). The institution of 'school' has been introduced in our civilized societies as the key institution to focus, foster and direct this natural process of growth and development in human engagements which lead children towards adulthood and becoming citizens in today's society.

On either side of the diagram, under Child and Adult, are listed some characteristic qualities and experiences with which each may regard themselves and the other. What they are aware of as they interact affects their interaction. As they look towards the world inhabited by adults, children have a natural sense of adventure, trust, fear, hope and so on. Adults in their turn, when regarding children, feel that those young people need to learn about the traditions of society, to know how to be a member of the tribe or the nation, know how to work productively, to understand the importance of the beliefs and values of the adult world, and so on. There is no guarantee, as they meet each other, that whatever is uppermost in the mind of one is also in the awareness of the other. Both participants are affected by the nature of their engagement.

As in the family, so in school: these processes are present in every school and in every encounter between adults and children. They take place as we encounter each other one-to-one and also in groups. The energy that fuels the processes comes from awareness by both adults and children that the qualities of the child need to be transformed into those of the adult within the same human person and this inevitably results in tensions between the generations which can be creative. It is obvious that at the same time as children reach out to the adult perspective, adults need to be in touch both with their own capacity to continue to be adventurous, playful, ambitious and so on, but also to be ready to find out the child's perspective: if they lose touch with these in themselves, the seeds of destructive tension are sown.

Authors' Comment: Witness a mother concerned about her 7-year old son's behaviour at table. She sees a boy who is behaving badly because he seems to be simply playing with his food; he feels that he is aware of a new idea about the world that has struck him. To her, he is a disappointment because she wants a well-behaved son; to him, his mother seems to be frustrating his following through the idea in his mind. How they resolve the tension will make one small contribution to the maturity of both of them.

Or again, Peter, aged 5, was with his grandfather watching a rugby match. The grandfather was a somewhat fervent Christian. At a critical moment in the game Peter turned and said 'Grandpa, can you kill God?' Feeling that this was a key moment in Peter's religious development and also feeling the heat of the moment in the game, Grandpa did not stop to ask how such an question had come to Peter's mind, but launched into a thumbnail account of the crucifixion and the resurrection, and their meaning. When he recounted this moment to Peter's parents they burst out laughing. Peter had recently been watching the DVD 'Hercules' and his question had been about the cartoon and whether or not Hercules could have killed Zeus; in their view deeper theological questions were not at the surface of the boy's mind.

The four developmental processes we have teased out and located in the Reed Rainbow are:

Initiation: models for behaviour and for making relationships.

Education: the possession of knowledge and skills about life, work, and the world.

Maturation: ways of understanding oneself in the context of a widening society.

Transformation: glimpses of unexpected energy, self-honed, which leads to the re-framing of their worlds.

Each process is followed by a characteristic development of experience.

- Initiation leads to *belonging*, as pupils take up their position as members of a society which they can understand, with their rights and obligations.
- Education leads to *learning* as pupils master the unknown in facing the world's challenges using their knowledge, understanding and capacity to communicate, finding enrichment of life, and growing capacities to work with the skills they acquire.
- Maturation leads to *empowerment* as pupils use their physical, mental and psychological powers to handle stress and conflict, learning to exercise their authority in taking up their corporate responsibilities in the running of their society.
- Transformation leads to *envisioning* as pupils take risks in trying to implement their dreams, hopes and beliefs both for themselves and for society as they appreciate the wider opportunities before them.

Let us tease these four different processes out a little more in the following sections.

1. Initiation and belonging

We have defined this process as:

> *Initiation* – which provides models for behaviour and making relationships. We have made the point that initiation leads to *belonging*. As pupils take up their position as members of a school society which they understand, with their rights and obligations within it, this provides the basis for belonging to the larger society within which the school exists.

We have evidence from the church schools study that feeling that one had been initiated and had a sense of belonging to the school was an important factor in the transformation. As one teacher said:

There is a sense of loyalty pervading the school, and pride, I think the pupils feel included because they are consulted and they have seen the improvements happen which benefited them.

There was that group of pupils who expressed their sense of belonging:

When asked what they thought the head's motivation was, a group of students responded instantaneously, 'us'.

Belonging is fundamental to all human life from the beginning.[3] The baby's first experience of belonging is to a person, the mother; but steadily, the sense grows of belonging to something more – father, siblings, grandparents, cousins and so on, which begins to add up to belonging to a 'family'. This capacity to belong corporately will be tested (and hopefully extended) as the child finds friends and moves on through school. Part of the significance of the structures of schooling is that the child is invited to belong to increasingly complex groupings, providing experiences from which to learn to manage one's belonging to groups, institutions and, as one grows up, society as a whole.

2. Education and learning

This is the process which we intuitively bring into focus when we think about schools. This is about what happens in the classroom, the laboratory, the gymnasium and on the playing field. This process is about subjects, knowledge and skill development. The adults here take the role of 'teacher' and 'classroom assistant'. The experience is shaped by the curriculum, tests and examinations. The focus is mainly upon mental activity and skill development. As two pupils and a teacher, quoted earlier, said:

I believe most students are motivated to work better because the teachers want to teach the pupils. I think this is down to the headteacher as I know he has meetings with staff every morning.
Pupil

School has become a place to work hard and play hard. **Pupil**

> *The headteacher has developed a culture of strengthening the pupils' belief in their own abilities, she has expected improved teaching standards and has been able to make firm decisions if the standards are not maintained. She is well aware of the need to develop links with both local business and national groups to address an improvement in opportunities offered both to and from pupils.*
> **Teacher**

Recognizing that effective learning takes place when pupils and teachers form a partnership, we quoted a head earlier who said:

> *We try to create young people who have a mind-set about themselves and the institution so that they can become learners. If you've got pupils who feel positive about themselves and about learning they can go to class to be partners with the teachers.*

There are many factors, most of which have been written about endlessly, but a small incident can illustrate some issues involved in the complexity of learning in a classroom.

Authors' Comment: As a school governor, I periodically 'track' a pupil through a day, to get a feel of what it is like in our classrooms from the pupil's point of view. I was with Sebastian, a boy in Year 8 whom the head had suggested I should track. I was told that Sebastian had the ability to go to university, but that he could be a handful in the classroom. We were in an English lesson: the teacher – who was fairly new into teaching – was writing words up on the board and asking students to write definitions in their books. After a few moments she asked for examples of the definitions children had written and excited pupils put up their hands. Sebastian was not all that excited so, perhaps in deference to me sitting beside him, he did put up his hand. A girl on the other side of the class was invited to offer what she had written. Of course it differed from what Sebastian had written, as did two other definitions that pupils offered.

Sebastian started laboriously rubbing out what he had written, while trying to remember what the other definitions were. He did not believe me when I told him that his definition was perfectly good, though different: not being a teacher of English, in his eyes I had no authority to comment on what he had done. In the meantime, new words were being pointed to and new definitions were being offered: Sebastian was steadily falling behind as he rubbed out and tried to write in the 'right' versions. Those pupils whose definitions were accepted must have learned about those words and their English improved as a result, but Sebastian was in a different position. It is doubtful if his English did improve in that lesson. Other things certainly took place, but not the advancement of his skill in English.

The example of Sebastian reflects the general anxiety in today's society about the process of subject learning and skill (the orange strand), which is expressed not only in league tables, but in television programmes such as *That'll Teach 'Em*, broadcast in 2003 and *That'll Teach 'Em Too*, broadcast in 2005, which compare life and achievement in schools using 1950s methods of teaching with life and achievement in the 21st century. So we make ourselves anxious by asking. Do children really learn as much as they 'should' in today's schools? Were the old-fashioned ways of teaching better at delivering 'learning'?

3. Maturation and empowering

Diagram 1 indicates levels of what happens in schools. Every school has different possibilities, pressures or competencies which may constrain them from enhancing adequately (which does not mean 'equally') all four of these processes. Some might think that this is about 'behaviour' and in a sense it is, but it is about *all* behaviour, not simply 'good' and 'bad' behaviour. It is about every aspect of how a human being responds to the dynamic context in which they find themselves. As one head we quoted above said:

The behaviour system is an act of grace.

Maturation and empowering affects everyone, staff and pupils. As the Diocesan Director of Education quoted earlier said of one school:

The behaviour management system is exceptional. It is higher than I've seen anywhere else (and I've been a head of three schools myself). Good behaviour is rewarded and bad behaviour is handled consistently and speedily. This is true across the whole staff. There is a theology underpinning what he does. I call it 'spiritual anthropology'. It's the belief in the nature of human beings: they need to know about high standards of right and wrong. ... This depends on an understanding of redemption and the possibility of forgiveness.

We have defined maturation and empowerment as being the process whereby human beings develop their powers to exercise authority in taking up their roles in their society. Here, we have in mind all aspects of personal power: psychological power and physical power. This strand is about children learning to handle stress, to deal with anger, to express affection; they learn to manage their own bodies, and to accept that physical success may involve tolerating a level of pain, and so on. This process happens in the microcosmic life of the classroom, the gym, the playing field and across the macrocosm of the school as whole. Indeed, an effective school provides opportunities for children to mature across the whole spectrum of school life.

In principle, most schools interpret the work of the tutor group as being the principal place to work on maturation and empowerment. However, just as language is developed across the whole curriculum, so also is this developmental strand. Of course, the fact is that the processes will take place anyway in some shape or form, but – just as those early tennis professionals developed racquet arms that were anything up to double the thickness of their non-racquet arms – the overall resulting 'shape' of the person may be distorted from what might have been developed under other conditions.

If we lay aside describing a tutor group session and return to the story of Sebastian to look at it from the point of view of what was happening in terms of the concepts of Maturation and Empowerment, new things come into view.

Authors' Comment continued: As Sebastian found his answers differed from those which were receiving approval from the English teacher, one could sense his growing frustration. Not only was he feeling that he was 'wrong' again and again, but his efforts to get things right were causing him to fall further and further behind. Had an adult not been sitting beside him, it is probable that his self-control would have cracked and he would have begun to look around the classroom for others in a similar state and together they would have begun to express their frustration by playing up, their immaturity combining as they sought to subvert the lesson. What was coming to the fore in that lesson was the possibility of some work being done on maturity and the capacity to manage oneself when feeling frustrated, within the subject context. There was a classroom assistant in the room, but she was immersed in helping 'good' students to learn English: she and the teacher seemed to be leaving the visiting adult to handle the maturation (behaviour?) question with the boy and the widening circle of others who shared his experience, which he was actually handicapped in doing directly without causing some confusion in the classroom.

'English' was continuing to be 'taught', though it may well have been the case that less and less 'English' was being 'learnt' as the frustration spread across the room. So, by the teacher's concentrating only on the Education and Learning strand and not taking the Maturation and Empowerment strand into account, there was a decreasing likelihood that Sebastian and other pupils like him would actually gain in their mastery of English.

If we also return to thinking about the yellow strand

of Initiation and Belonging, tacit messages were also being communicated to Sebastian. Since he seemed not to be answering 'correctly' (and his admittedly rather half-hearted putting up of his hand did not attract the teacher's attention) his feeling of being a full member of this class as a group was on the wane. The teacher was female and she tended to look for answers from girls, so he might have begun thinking that only girls 'belonged' there. The teacher was black as he was, but had she been white he might have begun to feel that he was also the 'wrong' colour to belong in there. But experiences like Sebastian's are probably reproduced day after day across our land.

4. Transformation and envisioning

As with the yellow, orange and red strands, the blue/purple one is also active all the time but may be more dormant in certain circumstances and activated at others. An inspiring teacher of a subject may enable children to envision themselves as software writers, chefs, authors and so on – exponents of the subjects they like in the world outside school. Such a teacher may take pupils much further in their pictures of what is possible for them and for the world.

In one school we know each class has an 'ambition tree' on its wall, created at the beginning of the year and showing the rich variety of ambitions each class contains. Here, the tutors tap into each child's vision of where they want to get to and how they need to transform themselves to get there. Combining it into a 'tree' demonstrates the rich variety present in the class and conveys something about what they might do to support one another in their progress together through the year. This activity gives them what we described earlier as 'glimpses of unexpected energy, self-honed, which leads to the re-framing of their worlds'. It enables them to engage with one another and their teacher to envision that it is worth their while to take risks as they try to implement their dreams, hopes and beliefs, both for themselves and for society.

However, children also live in a wider world and have feelings about that which have little to do with their own futures. They may find that their experience in school nurtures feelings of wanting to do something about global warming, animal experimentation, the plight of the starving or those ravaged by disease. This too might be handled at the level of tutoring, but larger gatherings of people are often more appropriate for this kind of development. It is this process which is placed in a wider frame by assembly and acts of worship. As teachers in the project schools remarked:

Worship and assembly are crucial. They are informative, educational and they invite reflection. Children take on board the message, and they talk about it afterwards.

The most effective assembly I have witnessed since arriving at the school was the morning after September 11th. The pupils demonstrated a real sense of understanding of the situation, sorrow, and a sense of belonging as a group.

And a pupil said:

I believe the assemblies allow the school to reflect on everyday life and how we can work to make it better.

We will have much more to say about this in Section 3.4 when we explore the technical issue of the function of worship in an institution.[4]

An overview of the significance of the Reed Rainbow in church schools

The challenge to all heads, whether in a community or church school is to offer the kind of leadership which enables all four strands of the Reed Rainbow to be integrated. This integration is possible when the headteacher works with a holistic picture of the school, seeing it as an organic enterprise with diverse parts interacting with each other in uninhibited ways. Of course, this raises the question of whether or not the head works on the assumption that *all* leadership is invested in the head; this is, of course, impossible from a practical point of view: to try to work as if it were is the gateway to failure. The head who works with the Rainbow in mind will see that leadership on any of the four strands can come from anywhere in the school, *including the pupils*.[5]

While all schools function in a social and political context, Church schools add an extra dimension to those contexts which can contribute to the school's transformation by placing the model of the Rainbow in the context of God's providence. This providence takes account of the strengthening of the human spirit, the widening of human concern for others, the deepening of human love for all and the awareness of human accountability to God. The outcome is the development of the virtues of faith, hope and love, in the promotion of the common good.[6]

Leading school transformation

Interviewing the heads, we obtained a view of what they were intending to achieve, their motivation and how they evaluated their own performance.

The three heads' *intentions* were to achieve the educational purpose of the school, by enabling pupils to learn and develop into responsible adults who could each contribute as citizens in their community in a way which reflected their own unique skills and capabilities. In all three, we found that what each head intended was given greater precision when we discussed practical issues in terms of the Reed Rainbow model. They could see how decisions and actions they had taken and which they planned could be located within the four processes, often prioritizing them in specific instances. Having a language in which to express their thinking more objectively, they could also see things on which they could do further work, involving other staff with greater freedom.

Their *motivation* came from their sense of a call to work for the well-being of their pupils whatever their situation, strengthened by their insight and steadfastness through relying on God's grace and power. They judged themselves against their capacity both to understand what they were seeking to do and in terms of their determination to take risks in carrying out what they saw to be their duty.

They each evaluated their own *performance* in terms of engaging with the school as a whole. In particular they took initiatives which encouraged the children to be responsible for themselves as pupils so that in each school the focus was shifted from (bad) *behaviour* to *learning* (good behaviour). In terms of the Reed Rainbow, they saw the ways in which children's growth and development take place in the children's minds, bodies and hearts.

When they arrived at their schools they accepted the judgements of Ofsted and other reports on the quality of teaching and behaviour, recognizing their own responsibility for working with their current staff and pupils. They developed their business plans, bearing in mind that it was the children and adults who were present in this school who needed leading to a new state of being. They were not there simply to transform a 'school' by getting rid of those who caused concern, but to enable each person in the school to raise their own achievement in the new context. This challenge provided hope to everyone involved, including the heads themselves.

So they set about changing the conditions of the school to focus on what mattered. In every case, their immediate action on taking up their positions as headteachers was to start this process off by introducing changes in school uniform, making school buildings more attractive whether it be the reception area, removing graffiti or painting toilets – all ways of encouraging pupils to be responsible for their behaviour.

A critical factor was their reaction to previous and current Ofsted reports. The heads saw their own responsibility in this. Accepting the validity of the judgements on the quality of lessons and results, they did not devalue their current staff or pupils, but developed and implemented business plans which challenged them, but also which gave them all hope.

A definition of a Christian leader which relates to these three heads has been offered by Henry J Nouwen:

> *A Christian leader is a person of hope, whose strength is based neither on self-confidence derived from their personality, nor on specific expectation of the future, but on a promise given them.*[7]

These heads were responding to the promise that God loved each of the children in their school, wished the best for them both in the present and in the future, and would provide all the necessary resources to enable that to happen. The heads' wish was to serve the children so that they could have viable and fulfilling futures; they did not believe that God's promise was simply to save the school itself, come what may. As one head said:

> *I have faced all sorts of difficulties and when I find myself at the end of my tether I pray, 'God, you called me here, what are you going to do about this situation?' God has never let me down. An early prayer was that if God had called me to close the school down that I should be able to do that with dignity. I now know that it was not for closure that I came but for a task which has not yet ended.*

Role as a dynamic process of self-disciplined behaviour

Though human beings are naturally institution-building beings, for any institution to function, human beings need to find ways of getting involved with each other, the physical and other resources that make up the whole. This does not happen in an arbitrary or random way. Rational and irrational processes combine to affect what actually happens. The link between the person and the institution through which involvement and, at best, commitment is achieved is called *'role'*.[8]

Our underlying thought is that the headteachers have each been able to discipline their behaviour as persons so as to implement their intentions in their schools, though to different degrees, depending on where they started. We call this discipline of their behaviour the process of working in role for the benefit of the school system (see Section 3.2), and we now wish to explore how they were able to *find* and *make* and *take* their roles in their work.

Finding the role

On being appointed to a position in an institution – in this instance as a headteacher in a school by the governing body – the person faces the question, whether articulated or not,

> *'Do I consider that I can discover how to behave as a headteacher so that I can do an effective job to fit the school to achieve its purpose?'*

What follows is to work out the *purpose* of this school, to become sensitive to its ethos and *culture*, to assess its *reputation* and the potentiality of its *resources*. The head does this by engaging with staff members and pupils, others in the school and the local community. The new headteacher then finds out whether the values of the school and its structure provide a space within which he or she wants to work, and a place from which to tackle the challenge and opportunity in a complex situation.

Whether or not their first experience of the school corresponds to what was said by the governors at the appointment, what Ofsted reports contained or anyone else has told them, if the headteacher accepts the challenge, then in technical terms, we conclude that the head has *'found the role'*, that is, they can see there is scope for him/her to behave/perform/work in that school as headteacher.

Making the role

The head is then faced with the task of *understanding the institution*, how its purpose is embodied in its structure, what resources are available and what capacities are brought to the school by all the people – children and adults – who work, study, teach and learn there. Knowing there is a role to be found, they set about *'making the role'*, that is, working out how to behave. As they do this, they relate their previous experience and knowledge to the dynamics of their new experiences. Their own behaviour contributes to these dynamics as other senior staff, teachers, pupils, parents and others begin to react and respond to their ideas and decisions.

The task of the headteacher is to discipline their own behaviour, being ready to take control of themselves in the changing circumstances, whether positively or negatively experienced. The self-discipline needs to be carried out in the world of reality, based on the capability of distinguishing what is actually happening from rumours, gossip and fantasy.

In considering this discipline, the three headteachers saw that they needed to work at a number of levels.

- The first level was to be sensitive to the children in this school and to believe in them, always keeping them in focus.

- The second was to be able to motivate and to give leadership to the staff.

- The third level is to manage the structure of the school so they could make the best use of their resources, with the support of the governors.

- The next level was to know how to interact with the community (especially, the LEA, the Church, the parents and other schools) to obtain new resources and support from that community in achieving it.

- The ultimate, and most significant level in a church school was to see the whole thing as part of God's purpose which is expressed through Jesus Christ's mission to humanity of creativity, redeeming love and justice.

Such disciplined behaviour, expressing the actual felt experience of the headteacher in his/her multiple relations, can be learned. Conceptual frameworks of human behaviour can enable the headteacher to develop and test hypotheses about what is real in the school and the consequences for everyone, including him/herself. This framework was used by the Grubb Institute staff in their research in the schools. By practising leadership skills, the headteacher begins to occupy the position of head with more assurance, while being even more conscious of the risky nature of leadership where changing circumstances are keeping them on their toes. As they make decisions, they try to manage the uncertainties they experience in themselves. This process of controlling one's own behaviour is described as *'making the role'* so that the school becomes the centre of their action.

Taking the role

The headteacher is now ready to act with the confidence that what they are doing is *for the benefit of the school* as a whole. What is to the benefit of the school can only be judged by relating the school to its place in society, by its contribution to the processes of the development of the child to adulthood. What *everyone* in the school experiences is the head's behaviour (which will include the impact of their decisions), while only some people hear what the head says. So, in taking the role, the head behaves in ways that demonstrate to the whole school what they believe what it means to belong to this school, what learning is about, what it is to behave maturely in the conditions that prevail within it, and what their ideas are about the world in which the school is placed, including what it can contribute to transforming that world.

The process of finding, making and taking a role is an iterative process. Once it has been taken, situations change so it needs to be re-found, re-made and re-taken. And, as the head takes their role with greater and greater precision, others – children and adults – in their turn can find, make and take their roles in the school.

Jill Clough comments: A head may find that this iterative process is hard for staff colleagues to grasp. As the head responds to contextual changes, these may be interpreted as unnecessary changes and seen as signs of the head's restlessness and inconsistency. In the normal climate of shifting contexts, what needs to be held constant is the idea of the purpose of the school. It is the constant idea of what the school is for that provides the stable container for people's anxieties about continual change.

During the initial periods of *finding* the role of headteacher and *making* the role, the headteacher has, of necessity, been taking action. However, the first two steps can affirm the head in the rightness of his/her behaviour in taking calculated risks, so that others can respond positively to what is being said and done by the head and see how they, in their turn, can also handle any negativity in the situation. With this awareness, the headteacher is able to see the moments of opportunity to act for the best results, as well as handling the inevitable setbacks creatively. In the hectic life of the head, timing now becomes more significant. This is the third step. After finding the role and making the role, the headteacher is now fully *'taking the role'.*

This three-step process of learning effective behaviour by the headteacher is no guarantee that everyone will agree with what they are doing or that the head will become popular by doing it. However, it does enable the head to work with integrity because they know that they are working for the good of the school as a whole and all its members. Therefore, they can be more motivated as leader to provide opportunities for the well-being of the pupils, staff and other stakeholders.

As will be apparent, the more one is taking the role, the more one is finding it, the more one is making it, and then the more one can have confidence in taking it. It is a continuous dynamic process where the 'shape' of the role is always subject to change as circumstances change.

Jill Clough comments: Once you have found the role, the issue that staff and pupils are confronted with is whether what you are doing is for you or for the school. When they are not certain, you have a problem; but if you are sure in yourself, they can come to see that you are doing it for the benefit of the school and the pupils, then they will come to trust you and follow you.

Taking a role is a practical way of achieving one's desire as a person by integrating it with the purpose of the school, without confusing one with the other. The principle applies to everyone in the school system. In this book, we have generally referred to people by naming their position. For example we have identified the educationally qualified adult appointed to the position to lead and manage the school as the 'headteacher', and the children attending school to be educated as 'pupils', and other qualified adults as 'staff' or 'support staff'. Strictly speaking, on joining or attending any system on any day, that particular person *takes a position*, e.g. headteacher, pupil, staff; it is then their responsibility to learn how to behave in that position in that school on that day so as to contribute to the furtherance of the school's purpose as a whole, not simply to satisfy their own impulses.

To the extent that the headteacher finds, makes and takes the role that others in the school can understand and respond to, they – the children and the adults – will be able to take their own roles as 'pupil', 'learner', 'teacher', 'support staff' and 'governor'. This is a vital part of the active leadership of the head.

The drive of transformative behaviour – power and authority

To understand the driving force behind the leadership of the three headteachers requires the exploration of their personal and professional qualities. Power and authority are facts of life in all working institutions. In those institutions where one group of people is of necessity dependent upon another, the way those in leadership positions use their power has major implications for how the other group feels and can function. Patients in a hospital depend on the medical and nursing staff to use their power. However, most patients are grown up and have experiences of the world and a degree of self-knowledge which enables them to manage themselves as patients; it is the resources of the medical, surgical and other skills that differentiate those patients from staff. In a school, most children are less experienced, lacking in knowledge and may be smaller than their teachers.[9] Their dependence on the school staff is great. This means that the way power and authority are understood and used in a school by the head and teachers is critical to how the four processes described in the Reed Rainbow are worked at.

In this book we define *power* as an attribute or property of the *person*. This is particularly important as the headteacher gets things done. The value of their actions is assessed by the consequent effect on the headteacher personally and upon their relations with others. We describe authority as power which has been legitimated by the other relevant members of the school by their experiencing what happens as being exercised for their benefit, thus making the school fit for its purpose. This is achieved when the headteacher is able to discipline his/her own behaviour by working in role. *Authority* in a school is therefore defined as an attribute of the *role* of the headteacher and, from that, an attribute of the roles of 'teacher' and 'pupil'.

Our working hypothesis is that, to different degrees, the three headteachers' professionalism and their Christian faith gave them the inspiration and direction *to work in role* so as to exercise authority in their schools. This gave freedom to everyone else to find, make and take their roles and thus, in their own terms, to work with authority whether they were child or adult. We recognize that there are other ways of learning to work in role than through Christian beliefs; what we do here is to illustrate how it worked for these headteachers, a major factor being their consistency in legitimizing different types of power.

Drawing on our work with leaders of other institutions over many years, we now *classify five different types of power*. We describe them here in turn and show how, when power is legitimated, it is deployed as authority. The results are then dramatically different. At any one time, a person is likely to be employing more than one type of power. However, in the first instance, we will focus on them one at a time.

Five types of power and their legitimization as authority

1. *Experiential Power (Px)* is the power that each person has, based on their life experience of learning, skills, qualifications and know-how combined with resources of intelligence, character and temperament to develop their competence. This power is intrinsic and theoretically is always available though when in new, oppressive or strange situations, the person may lose touch with their capacities and feel 'de-skilled'. The exertion of this power fosters the headteacher's own reputation and ambitions which may be experienced by others as good and noble, or bad and oppressive, depending upon which other powers are being exerted at the time.

Where Experiential Power is being deployed by the headteacher working in role for the well-being and benefit of the institution – the school – it is legitimated as *authority*, it enhances the school and its achievements. It depends on the head having sufficient competence (*Px*) both to define the school's purpose for its stakeholders and to understand its structure.

The competence of the three heads enabled them to understand the different purposes of their schools in their specific predicaments, with their past levels of performance and poor reputations which the heads faced initially. As we have shown, they were able to discover how to find, make and take their headteacher roles so they could focus on the benefit of the school. They exercised *authority* in working with staff to teach the pupils.

This authority was recognized in these schools by the pupils, expressed by one boy when he said:

The most important thing the head has done is to take charge, he has begun and still is rewarding students for hard work.

By definition, children have much less Experiential Power than the adults in the world and in school. However, they are not entirely lacking in it and where the head and the teachers recognize how children struggle to find, make and take their authority in their roles as pupils in the school, they can find freedom to make full use of all the resources of the school. A pupil in one of the schools had grasped this about the head:

> *The head's motivation is us! He cares about us, about trying to improve things and he provides new facilities. He asks our opinions.*

2. *Official Power (Po)* is the power a person has by virtue of the title of their position within the school as a headteacher in a local community. Without knowing the person or even meeting them, the 'headteacher' can be felt as a threat by a pupil, and often is so exploited by members of staff to control their class, 'I'll send you to the headteacher.' Official power can function in this negative way regardless of the person of the head, but it can also be used by the headteacher or staff negatively by deliberately promoting their image in the school as powerful and as one who says 'I've heard about you . . . '.

Headteachers can consciously use their Official Power for the benefit of the school so that it becomes *authority*. A news reporter remarked to one head about her appearance that '*she did not look like the head of a failing school*' and received the tart reply '*I always dress like this – in case I meet the Queen.*' The head was indicating that the school merited that level of dressing and in the head's mind it was not a 'failing school', but one she was proud of. A governor of another school remarked on the way parents saw the head: '*They feel that here is a humble, not an overbearing person, but someone with great competence.*'

All three headteachers greeted their pupils as they met together for worship which diminished the sense of remoteness and awe (Official Power), and by their subsequent behaviour then took their authority in the role of worshipper alongside them.

On the occasion of the induction of a new Provost to the local cathedral when local pupils were being asked to assist in the service, the head, on hearing that because of its bad reputation the only Church of England secondary school was being ignored in favour of non-church schools, protested to the Bishop, who then changed his mind and invited them to take part. Here the head used her Official Power for the benefit of the school which legitimized it as exercising *authority*. In order to participate, some pupils even borrowed other pupils' shoes for the occasion. They presented themselves so well at the induction that they have since been invited by the Provost to take part in special cathedral services in future. This successful exercise of authority, based on Official Power has had a considerable influence on the pupils' self-esteem, and their school's reputation is being gradually enhanced in the community.

3. *Instrumental Power (Pi)* is the power of deploying the resources which a headteacher can use to carry out their purpose. Resources include the school premises and equipment, the staff and the finances to run the school. Instrumental Power can be used in times of hardship to control people and school activities, or to promote the reputation and self-image of the headteacher.

In the project schools, their headteachers saw opportunities to use Instrumental Power legitimately. One headteacher, as soon as possible after his appointment, used his limited finances to recondition the toilets as a way of enabling pupils believe they were cared for and respected. Another head, on hearing that the school's toilets had been trashed, immediately called a school assembly, and expressed his anger in describing what had been done and asking the perpetrators to come and confess to him. They did. It was an instance where pupils experienced him using his *authority* in role based on Instrumental Power for their interests.

All three heads worked with their senior managers and consulted their staff before taking decisions which affected them, so that their use of Instrumental Power was supportive of their work. The head's exercise of authority based on Instrumental Power then freed up staff and others to take authority for themselves. A good example was the way one school introduced new uniform to pupils so that as a result all of them were wearing it after three days despite the initial protests from parents and the local education authority; the fact was that as parents they had been consulted and their problems discussed and, where necessary, costs were subsidized by the school.

4. *Projected Power (Pp)* is the power which is attributed to the headteacher by others who believe they will either look after them (Positive Projected Power – P+p), or alternatively, be 'out to get them' (Negative Projected Power – P-p). Positive Power is necessary for a head to be a leader. The psychological process is largely unconscious and comes from 'splitting', where pupils and staff entrust their 'good parts' to the head and keep the 'bad parts'. If this becomes out of balance, others lose self-respect/confidence or put (project) their bad points onto someone else to blame them, e.g. to dislike a teacher, or onto a group of pupils different from themselves which, if from other races, can result in racism (Negative Projected Power).

If headteachers are unaware of the Positive Projected Power process going on around them, they can come to believe they are doing a better job than in fact they are, and become 'larger than life' in their own opinion. Using the Projected Power available to them, they can come to unrealistic attitudes and 'boss' members of staff and pupils. Moreover, they can be over-optimistic about what is going on in the school. In any case, projected power leaves them focusing on themselves rather than on the realities of the school.

Headteachers who are working in role, handle projections very differently. They do not count on being popular, so if they have Negative Projected Power they are not overwhelmed by the negativity and try to understand what it tells them about the state of the school as a whole, not about themselves as persons. Such heads, who are aware of Positive Projected Power, in accepting the projection see themselves as serving the school. They attribute their 'good' feelings to the effective work with staff and pupils, and give the credit to others rather than to themselves. This leads to growing self-respect among pupils. A governor described this process in one school:

At the first Prize Giving the November after his arrival you could see his pride in the students and the joy in his face .... He shows that he esteems them and that gives them self-esteem.

Authority then comes easily, as everyone is working for the benefit of the school so there is no obvious resistance. This passing on of the success to others shows that to act with humility is the supreme expression of authority.

5. *Spiritual power (Ps)* is power experienced by a headteacher who has a strong belief in God. We distinguish this from those who have belief in the spirituality of human beings. That belief we consider to be based on their human experience with others and is classified as Experiential Power. Spiritual Power is reserved for those who consider they have had an encounter with God – the Other – which has affected their lives, and, in particular, we are concerned here with headteachers who have discovered Jesus Christ as the Son of God.

Christian headteachers are under pressure by some educationalists to keep their belief private to themselves. Some welcome this and see Christian faith in terms of their own salvation which they do not need to express in public. For them, their Spiritual Power is not legitimized. On the other hand, strong Christian personal faith causes some headteachers (and other staff) to feel they have the right overtly to try to 'win people for Jesus'. They may believe they are exercising authority in doing this they are mistaken. If they were in the market place or at an evangelistic rally, their boldness to speak in the name of the Gospel might be the work of authority; but in a school, with its purpose of education, it is not legitimized because the person has not taken up the role of headteacher in fitting the school for its purpose.

The pupils, teachers and governors in all three schools described their experience of the Spiritual Power of their head:

The head has a belief in his calling and vocation, and in the guidance of the Holy Spirit ... He professes his faith in an interesting and in no sense formidable way.

The head put Gospel values at the heart of the school, he makes frequent reference to these values when talking to staff and pupils.

He does not force Christianity upon pupils but encourages them to respect each other's beliefs.

He has strong beliefs and tries to reflect them in the way he runs the school.

In the section on worship, we showed how headteachers have evolved services of worship which are the heads' manner of expressing the purpose of the school in relation to God's love and purpose for humanity. Through these corporate acts the headteachers exercised spiritual *authority*, the legitimation of their Spiritual Power.

Authority and power in practice

While all the heads exercised power and authority, because some had been there a shorter time than others, they worked differentially. The head of one school was appointed in 1999; the heads of other two in 1996. In the first school, where there was urgency in getting out of Special Measures, the headteacher used power (Experiential Power, Official Power and Instrumental Power) in making things happen. The consequence was that, while greatly respected (Positive Projected Power) for her leadership and Christian faith, the staff of the school were not yet in a position to take over from her spiritual leadership. Though they respected her and the chaplain and valued their work, it was still comparatively early days. In one of the other two schools, where the head worked naturally as a manager (Experiential Power), the school responded to his use of authority and staff appreciated his concern for the pupils and their parents (Experiential Power) in winning them over to his policies. The Christian leadership was clear and firm but gentle in that the head was passionately *for* the pupils, 50% of whom came from Sikh families. In the third school, the head had skilfully used authority consistently (Official Power and Instrumental Power) so that his Christian faith was not only respected, but his spiritual leadership (using Spiritual Power) opened up new possibilities to the pupils. This head's example was powerful in drawing others to respond while experiencing the freedom which is bestowed when leaders behave with authority as distinct from power which constrains them.

A tentative working hypothesis about staff/head relations emerges from this brief analysis. When a head is first appointed, they establish themselves and are experienced by others as using power more than authority. This may be Experiential Power, Official Power, Instrumental Power or Positive Projected Power. If they do not use the power they have, other people with power may move in to fill what is seen as a vacuum. A sound working hypothesis is that failing schools are those in which many people may be exercising power of one sort or another (including children), but because there is no sense of legitimation through the school's shared purpose, energy is more likely to contribute to a vicious rather than a virtuous circle.

Jill Clough comments: In a school that has been failing, one of the experiences of a new head is that there are people who have got into the school to 'do things' to it. Many of these work with power, but without authority in the school and therefore have a great potential to undermine the head. One of the new head's first acts must be to move these people out.

A second phase follows when their policies are manifestly succeeding, when the headteacher can increasingly share their approach with staff and pupils who then experience them as using authority.

The third phase follows when the head's behaviour is transparent to all who experience authority as giving staff freedom to manage with authority themselves and for children to find, make and take their own roles as pupils and learners, at whatever stage in the school's life they may be.

Head/pupil relations are complex, because so much is mediated through staff. However, the pupils of all three schools in the study greatly benefited from the way their heads used authority and power, and their behaviour (if not yet their results) raised the reputation of their schools as the pupils demonstrated their self-esteem. This dignity was a reflection of pupils experiencing the authority of the head through their constant love and care for them. As one pupil said of the head: *She never gives up on you.*

The schools' transformations were therefore not just the result of competence and energy, but also of self-discipline, in this instance, due to the heads' willingness to follow Christ's way. They could work with the negative aspects of their schools and transform them, e.g. poor pupil behaviour, and weak professionalism of staff, so that the reputation of the school was changed from bad to good, becoming a place to which parents wanted to send their children.

3.2 Leading and managing systems

Schools, like all organizations, are places where many people come together to do things with one another. Everyone has their own idea of what they are seeking from the institution. To an outsider, most places of work are virtually unintelligible; even to insiders, institutions are often on the verge of sliding into chaos. Everyone, not least newly arrived headteachers, need something on which to base their understanding of the school. Past experience of similar institutions of the same kind can help; but they can also be a handicap, causing some of the unfamiliar to be screened out and the familiar imposed. This is one reason why heads who have been 'parachuted in' seldom leave long-term changes.

This section offers a coherent way of thinking about human beings in shared organizational settings. We begin with persons (children are persons too) and then build up into organizations, thinking of them as human systems of activity with a purpose. We return to the concept of role as a way of managing oneself and one's relatedness to others for the benefit of the system in which all are participants. We then explore how persons can be effectively bonded together in a shared enterprise by their leader, which they can join in with a sense of freedom.

In a sense, the effective head can be described as offering not *'the desire of the leadership, but the leadership of desire'*. The next three sections progressively build this up.

Working with experience – individually and corporately

As living beings, we all have experience. Our sense of our own identity grows from our experience, accumulated since birth, including our judgements about ourselves and how those relate to the judgements others make of us. Our behaviour reflects how we have been influenced by our experience of relations with others, but it would be unwise to say that it expresses what we have 'learned' from our experience. Some of our responses to circumstances may be more a case of conditioning than learning. It is said that a cat never sits on a hot stove twice – but then neither does it sit again on a cold one.

As human beings, we can discriminate between hot and cold stoves because we can reflect on what happens to us and around us; we are able to assess facts that we encounter, our relations with other people and our feelings about those; we can recall facts and feelings from our past, relating them to our present and predicting what may come in the future. Children's learning from birth to three or four years old is almost entirely derived from their experience. They learn to live skilfully, not by being formally taught, but from what happens as they engage with the world around them; they learn physical self-management, develop the capacity to speak, assess who is likely to be friendly and who seems threatening, begin to differentiate dangerous from safe situations. As they grow up, they begin to learn formally those more abstract skills that will be valuable as adults – language, followed by reading, writing, calculating, remembering facts, passing tests, making plans and so on. Learning from their experience may get less and less attention as they grow up, but does not become less and less important.

From the point of view of living skilfully in society, experience actually becomes more important. Understanding who we

SKOOB BOOKS (EST 1979)
The Brunswick, WC1N 1AE
020 7278 8760

[illegible]
[illegible]

Others [illegible]6.00

ITEMS 10
CASH [illegible]6.00

112,000 [illegible] Books
at WWW.SKOOB.COM
VAT 824882700

are, what our experience means and how we can engage with others to achieve purposes together is not learned from books or from teaching. To do this demands skill and, since adult life is lived not simply as individuals but corporately, learning in school prepares us to take part in the wider community which is the adult world.

The Reed Rainbow offers us a way of holding in our minds our experience of processes, but what that leaves open for further understanding is learning how to relate ourselves to our contexts. In today's culture of individualism we can be tempted to restrict the implications of the Reed Rainbow to individual personal development, as if what happens inside each one of us were the whole story. The heads in the church schools study all had a sense of working in role, interpreting their experience of the relations around them. They thought in terms of the 'school' which they saw as a human enterprise being created and recreated everyday by everyone who engaged with it. The 'school' was not simply an imagined thing existing in their own heads, but a form of elaborate 'dance' in which everyone took part together. The 'school' was created out of everyone's heads as each person – head, teachers, pupils, governors, parents and others – expressed in their behaviour towards each other how they experienced the 'school' and each other as participants in it. Living together in school demanded skill from everyone involved and a key area for children's learning is the development of that skill. It was evident that intuitively these three heads could live skilfully in school in ways which were communicated to others so that a shared enterprise emerged.

So, we need a device which enables us to interpret the experience and skill of living corporately, within organizations, interacting with each other in managed rather than arbitrary ways. We have already outlined the concept of role, but we now need to go further.

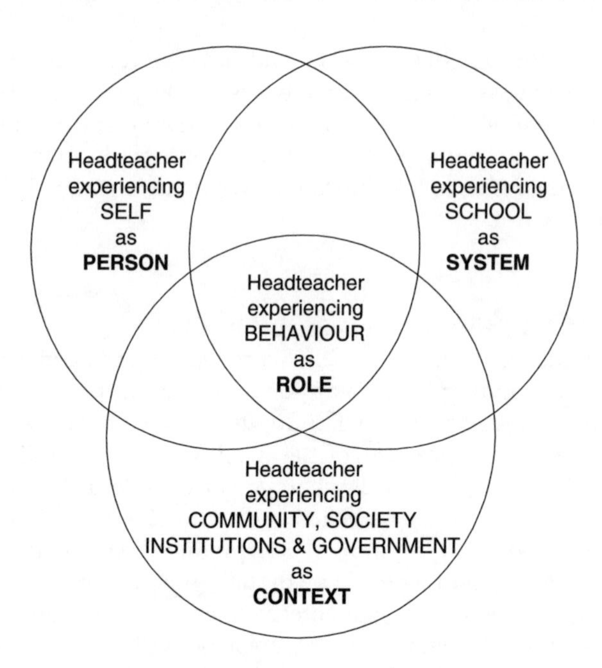

Figure 2: Interaction of key concepts.

Concepts of 'person', 'system', 'context' and 'role'

The model of *person, system, context* and *role* offers an integrated framework of behavioural, organizational and theological concepts. This has been developed by The Grubb Institute, through its research and assignments with personal and institutional clients across a wide spectrum of business and professional life. Diagram 2 summarizes key concepts and their interaction as applied to headteachers in church schools.

These key concepts of person, system, context and role are '*mental constructs*', i.e. these are ideas-in-the-mind formed by headteachers through their experiences in school life.[10] These four concepts are not the only concepts to sum up the experience of school life by the head. For example, the headteacher may experience self as individual, man, woman, adult, British, German *etc*. Also, the head may experience school as organization, as workplace, as community *etc*, and experience context as family, bureaucracy, politics *etc*. While person, system, context and role may not appear to be the most obvious concepts, we have chosen them because they are interdependent and they contribute to each other's working interpretation as we shall show in the following sections.

Because of our central interest in the leadership and management offered by the three heads in their different schools, each section will conclude with a note on its implication for the headteacher's leadership and management.

Person

To experience oneself as *person* the headteacher takes note of his/her interactions with other people, with the past, with the world (especially the educational world) and how those interactions are being felt – pleasant, unpleasant, hopeful, despairing, developmental, repressive *etc*. The headteacher as *person* then considers what to do in response to those interactions and the effect these are having upon their understanding and self-awareness. This is a continuous, ever varying process expressing the inner resources of the person, their character, intelligence, aspirations, energy and state of health. It is worth paying some attention to this aspect of personal development over a lifetime, using a simple diagram to clarify things.

Person can be represented diagrammatically to indicate the mental process of interaction between the inner world of the person, the outer world of the context and the school and the means by which as adult the process can be managed and outcomes planned. At birth, the infant is unable to distinguish itself from its context, particularly its mother, so we can represent this by a dotted circle, indicating the way self and context can blend into one another.

Within its skin the infant has feelings, reactions and desires. Hunger, pain, rage, satisfaction, joy, warmth, comfort and so on are all experienced, but it is hard to differentiate these from the

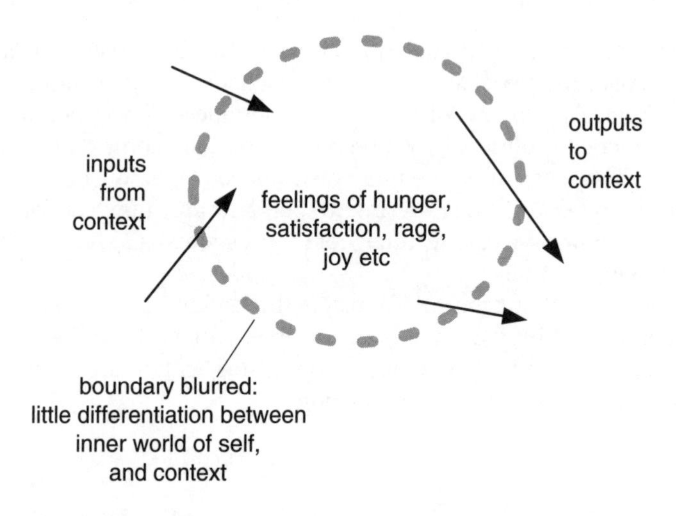

Figure 3: The inner world and context of the infant.

context. The baby's experience is simply of *being,* though that is only part of the story. The baby's sense of being is at first inextricably woven into how its mother feels, both in herself but also about the baby. As Susan Gerhardt puts it, *'The baby is an interactive project, not a self-powered one.*[11]' The infant's skill in managing the interaction is minimal to start with, its desire for something being expressed through tears and crying, but the skill begins to develop to new levels as the infant learns from experience that it has both an inner world and an outer world that provides it with a context, and that by its behaviour it can influence the interaction between the two. Smiles and cries of joy become part of the repertoire for achieving what one desires. This capacity to influence interactions can be represented in our diagram by firming up the psychic 'skin' or personal boundary in the diagram. We use a single line because at this stage there is not much conscious thought about the influencing – it may involve some level of skill, but it could not yet be described as 'managing' the interaction.

Interactions with siblings, parents and others in the family

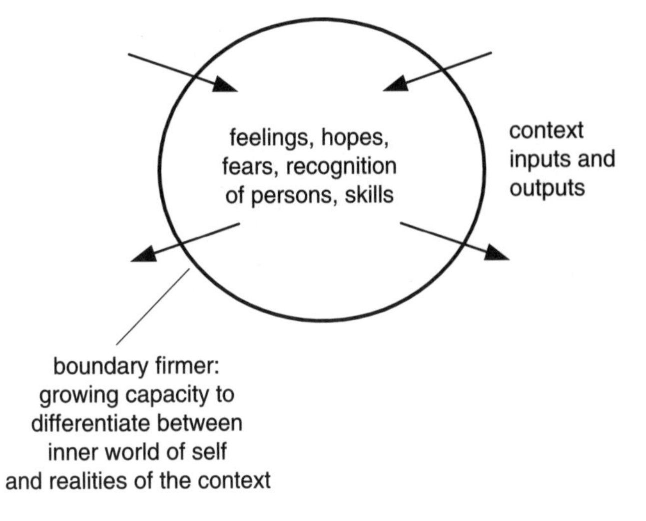

Figure 4: The child begins to differentiate between its inner world and its context.

provide the events and experiences from which the child learns that they can begin to be more skilful in handling their engagement with those around them. They become more aware of their desires and can choose to let their feelings erupt in a burst of joy or rage and to find that other people react in ways that they had hoped. As early as two years old they become aware of having thoughts – intangible things in their mind that they can choose to share with others or withhold so that no-one else has access to them. As Sue Gerhardt points out, the way the child's mother handles her own inner world provides the basis on which the child learns to handle their own internal processes.

At school, the circle of human beings with whom they interact expands and now includes people they may like or dislike, know well or only see around the place. Behaviour within the classroom, the playground and the school as a whole becomes something to which more attention needs to be paid because it is increasingly expected of one. Skill in 'self-management' in

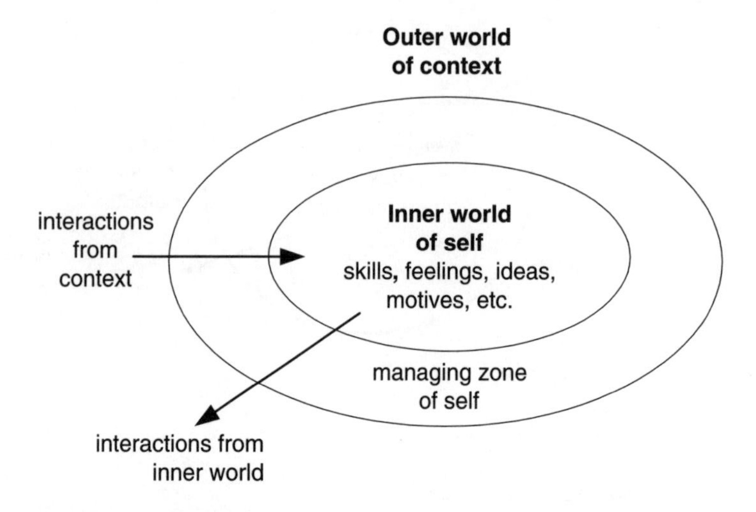

Figure 5: The person with the skill to manage interactions between inside and outside.

relation to one's desire is now being learned, mainly from experience but also as a result of rewards and corrections.

Once in school, the child begins to appreciate that whereas in the family the idea of some kind of shared or overarching purpose which takes precedence over desire virtually never occurs consciously – most families are simply about being – the collective culture of the school means that more attention is paid to *purpose,* which calls for a greater capacity to manage oneself in relation to why people have come together. *Purpose* is the shared intention which brings people together in order that all the different desires, cultures and beliefs which are brought in can work collaboratively towards a common objective. This means that as a person, the child now discovers that more and more conscious attention needs to be paid to self-management in relation to objectives. He or she learns that there is a skill to be developed about living together which is more than about getting one's own way.

The 'weak skin' which separated the baby and child from the outside world now needs to be developed and gradually strengthened, enabling the person to manage the way they relate to others, not simply to gain one's own desires, but to achieve the shared intentions from which all can benefit. Where, for a child, feelings would erupt spontaneously and desire be expressed uncontrolledly, as a mature adult, the person can decide whether or not *and how* to show any feelings or to reveal their desire. They learn to judge whether this is appropriate in the light of the purpose. At the same time, the adult monitors the interactions and feelings from others in the context, using their intermediate 'managing zone' to receive, adjust to, or decline the approaches and work of other people. Helping children and young people to learn this is one of the key skills of teachers in the long run, more important even than learning subjects and passing exams. As we will see later, the same skill principle can be applied to thinking about *system*.

Thus, as *person*, the headteacher is aware of their competencies, ambitions, beliefs, ideas and feelings and the necessary tensions through the relations with the complexity of people, artefacts and institutions of the external context. As person, they can respond to changes in these relations and express any differences of feelings and attitude to them. The skill they demonstrate in this is a key factor in what others learn from engaging with them in the school.

Their beliefs and values are significant factors here. A Christian headteacher will experience a resonance between their own personal beliefs about God and beliefs and views about how God is working in the school and the wider world. Interpreting these experiences by the headteacher behaving in role, is key to the distinctiveness of their leadership. This skill is what scripture refers to as *'wisdom'*.[12] A head with other religious beliefs – say a Jew or a Muslim – will apply their beliefs to find resonance with the context and will behave in ways that reflect that resonance. A politically motivated head will function in a similar way.

From this, it is evident that each *person* can be understood as being an intersecting point of a complicated net of relations, reaching out through time and space to people, institutions and other networks. If one is alert to being such an intersection, it influences how one uses power and authority and the ways one exercises leadership and management.

Implications I
Thinking of being in both a network and a structure

Leadership I
As *person*, the headteacher senses the possibilities for the future and is ready to take initiatives. Interactions with the school-in-the-mind will reflect personal qualities (Experiential Power) and the projections of others (Positive Projected Power and Negative Projected Power). This leadership relies on the network of relations and also is developed as fellow-workers – including pupils – grasp that they have a leader to follow.

Management I
As ***person***, the skill is the management of self – containing but not denying one's feelings and experience, but drawing on them as powerful resources in the changing dynamics of the situation, making oneself fit for the purpose of being headteacher.

Jill Clough comments: When you first go into a school as a new head you have to decide quickly what the expectations of you are. You bring with you memories of leadership in your previous schools (your own and that of your own previous heads) and you are tempted to read situations as if they were familiar to you, turning yourself into a person in a past context. This means that you misread how people relate to you. Your new pupils and staff have their memories too and will be reading you as if you were in some way linked to their past. Much of the necessary tension of the opening phase of one's time in the new school will be due to different pictures in everyone's minds about the role of this head in this school now; which will have implications for the idea of the roles of everyone else.

System

From very early in life, human beings naturally interpret their contexts in terms of systems, even if we are unaware of it. We intuitively perceive people grouped to carry out activities together: we discern boundaries around groups and sense ourselves as being in or out of those groupings. Every time we have a sense of 'us' and 'them', we draw a boundary and create in our minds a systemic relatedness. The issue facing leaders and managers is to be clear enough in their own heads about the boundaries, resources and structures of the system they are charged with so that they can convey them to others. From how the head draws the boundary, others can develop a sense of belonging in the school system which transcends personal likes and dislikes.

John Bazalgette remembers: A small group of boys was playing together in the street. The eldest was about 5 and the youngest something over 3. They had organized themselves into a little 'gang' with the eldest being the gang leader. They decided that the youngest should do something and the gang leader gave him an order. He refused. 'You must do it' he was told. 'No, I won't', he said. 'We'll beat you up', said the gang leader. 'All right, I'm not a member of the gang any longer', said the 3-year old. The capacity to recognize a system boundary was there already and with it the recognition that one is no longer subject to the rules and conventions if one is outside the system.

In experiencing the school as *system* the headteacher can be understood as assembling a range of their own experiences and

Figure 6: A management discussion.

organizing them inside his/her head to form a coherent mental construct of activities within a boundary. The headteacher outwardly sees the buildings, watches children growing up, going to classes, and playing, engages with staff in meetings, meets parents and governors, makes and receives phone calls, deals with letters and emails etc. All those are important aspects of school life which occur separately. The head, however, does not physically 'see' the entire school as one whole. The best possibility for them is to 'envisage' it, by trying to fit all the pieces together, to fill up any gaps and avoid overlapping and to give expression of that mental image so that others can perceive it too. Sometimes such things as governor's meetings and senior staff meetings can face difficulties because others present put the same pieces together differently from each other and from the headteacher, which can lead to breakdown in understanding between them. This can become very serious and is common in cases where a school is performing poorly.

The communication problem can be illustrated by Diagrams 6 and 7.

The head, after discussing an issue with a teacher, agrees what the latter will do about it. Afterwards the head is dismayed to hear that the teacher did something quite different from what

Figure 7: Different ideas in the mind.

the head thought they had decided together. The mistake can be better understood if the 'shape' of the school assembled together by the head was (say) 'triangular' and the shape for the teacher was 'square' (Diagram 7).

In discussion, they had accordingly misinterpreted what each was saying, leading to the muddle. This example shows the need for the head to have a working model in-the-mind which can be shared by exploration throughout the school, so that staff (especially) can experience for themselves the *system* in the way the headteacher does, even if they disagree about it. Of course, the same principle applies to engagements between pupils and teachers.

The difference between these working models in-the-mind can be interpreted by the use of two mental constructs, the *institution-in-the-mind* and the *organization-in-the-mind*.

An institution has a *specific existence*, though the nature of the evidence of its existence may not be obvious. For example, a school exists as a building with people, lessons, technology, resources, but each pupil and member of staff may have a different idea of what it is about because of their feelings and experiences of it, that is, the school as an institution exists in-the-mind. It exists in the minds of people within the school and outside it, representing a wide range of attitudes, feelings, memories and ideals. These have both conscious and unconscious dimensions which interact and affect how people engage with the school both from inside and from outside.

Authors' Comment: An issue which faith schools face, whether they be Church of England, Roman Catholic, Jewish or Muslim schools, is a strongly held belief that they are 'exclusive', designed either to corral children into a belief or covertly to select them to obtain advantage over others in the community. This is an example of 'institution-in-the-mind' which can be sufficiently powerful over time to become a self-fulfilling view, whatever may be the present realities of the school. This was an issue faced by the three schools in this study, though each of them, both in practice and intention, saw themselves as serving their whole local community inclusively.

Similarly an *organization*, comprising the complex set of relationships in the school necessary to plan and carry out its aspirations, is in-the-mind. The organizational structure, role relations, performance indicators, timetable and so on, show how the institution has been designed to achieve something – the aim.

A stranger to a school may be aware of staff and children in rooms for a while, but when they hustle from one place to another, the visitor can make little sense of what is happening. The head can instantly interpret it, because their *organization-in-the-mind* has been developed to carry out the purpose of the *institution-in-the-mind*. Both these concepts are aspects of the school system and are part of the mental make-up of everyone connected with it.

A basic system is also constructed of other concepts. The *aim* gives the reason why the school exists in its context; the *activities or processes* of the pupils and staff are designed to achieve the aim; the *boundaries* between different activities and resources of time, place and persons ('in' class, 'out' of class, 'in' school, 'out' of school) are there to enable those processes to be regulated and differentiated from the *context* in which the school is operating,

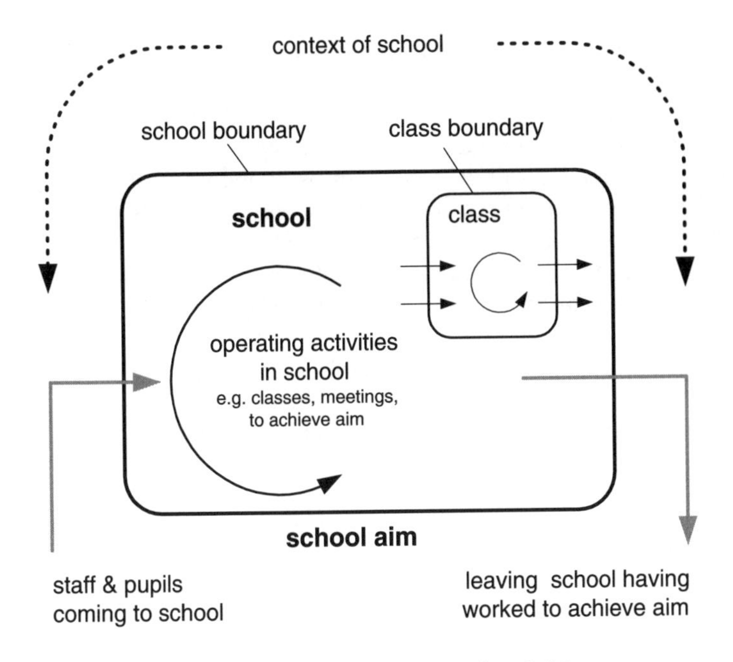

Figure 8: School as a system of activities.

from which the pupils and staff come. These concepts apply both to whole systems and their sub-systems.

> **Authors' Comment:** Imagine a boy on a canal bank during a school day, with his rod and jam-jar. Is he truanting? Not if he is carrying out a biology project. The system of the class is thus not restricted to physical classroom or laboratory, but as an idea-in-the-mind, locates him within the work of the school even if he is a long way away from the school buildings.

Because school works intermittently, staff and children alternate daily between going to school and going home. So like a living, breathing organism, the school as a system continually interacts with its environment in a vast range of different ways.

In showing the school as a system, in Diagram 8 a class is shown as one sub-system. There are many more sub-systems including registration of tutor groups, worship, staff meetings, governor's meetings, disciplinary meetings *etc.* Each of these can be located within the *system of activities*.

However, not all these sub-systems are *operating* systems contributing directly to the aim of the school. The headteacher will also be aware of working with and experiencing *managing sub-systems* (Senior Leadership Team meetings, subject team meetings, staff meetings *etc*), *service sub-systems* (canteen, premises management, secretarial services *etc*) and *control sub-systems* (finance, Inset *etc*). All these sub-systems require the head to construct in his/her own inner world a way of thinking about them both separately and together, to be able to envision the school system 'holistically', the whole and parts together. As the head finds ways to articulate and express their institution-in-the-mind and their organization-in-the-mind, pupils and teachers can buy into them and can begin to devote their efforts to work with the head for the benefit of the school.

Whereas the experience of *person* enables the head to see the school as a complex series of *networks*, experience of *system* enables the school to be understood as a *corporate* entity or body. Thinking corporately enables the head to see how each sub-system reflects the whole system in its functioning, and how the total system in turn reflects each of the sub-systems. Hence, the everyday remark, 'the whole is greater than the sum of its parts'.

A Christian head would see the school as a structure, within which the Spirit of God can be seen at work, holding together the everyday events of the school's life. Similarly, though the nature of their God will differ from the Christian's view of God revealed through Jesus Christ, a head with different religious beliefs would seek to discern how their deity is expressed in the realities of life in the school. In both cases the wisdom of the head will constantly be called into play as each day progresses.

Implications II
Thinking in terms of system, boundary and context.

Leadership II
Experience of the school as *system* can evoke in the head an intuitive sense of purpose. It may foster work on the specific definition of the aim of the whole school system and the aim of the sub-systems by working with those immediately involved. Leaders move from thinking 'my' to talking about 'our' in this process. Here, the head is thinking in terms of Official Power (*Po*) and Instrumental Power (*Pi*). The skill of good leadership is to work in the world of reality with what is possible, not in the dream world of impossible achievements. Such leadership encourages and empowers staff to be engaged in their work, as they find their own *Po* and *Pi* and to use them skilfully.

Management II
The emergence of the outline of the system requires management to assess available resources, then deploy them and ensure they are managed to enable the operation and support systems to be fit for their purposes. Here the head uses Instrumental Power (*Pi*) to make things happen.

Jill Clough comments: Senior staff can sometimes tell their head, 'Something's going wrong with your school.' For the head simply to talk of 'our' and 'we' is not enough: it needs to be behaved and therefore experienced by others. In this way, your leadership's credibility and realism is tested. This shows up most clearly when decisions about the use of resources are on the agenda because this is a test of the head's ability to think practically.

Context

The headteacher's experience of *context* constitutes the *outer* world of the school system, in the same way as the operating activities and sub-systems form the *inner* world of the system.

The context generates a number of formal and legal relations between the school and other systems. For example, families, through children and parents, Local Education Authorities through advisers, officers, grants and regulations, Department for Education and Skills through policies, National Curriculum, directives and grants, Ofsted through inspection and accountability, business through partnerships and support, primary schools as sources of new pupils, other local schools through co-operation in joint projects, FE colleges and universities through future opportunities and conditions *etc.* For Church of England schools, the headteacher has support and guidance and, through its Diocesan Board of Education Adviser, specialist advice, inspection and regulations. Apart from these formal relations, there are other organizations embodying the cultures of the community through its parish, social, commercial and sporting interactions with the school and its members. They represent informal relations from which comes the support of volunteers, and which provide the local and national media for public relations and recruitment of staff.

All these relations with external systems need to be competently managed to benefit the school and its purpose, and need to be incorporated into the headteacher's mental image of the school, into his/her extended *organization-in-the-mind* at a conscious level. Along with this, the cultural values, ethical norms, political ideals and religious beliefs are being absorbed by the headteacher. The feelings and realities generated by these influences lead to a deeper and unconscious image of *the institution-in-the-mind*.

The very existence of the school depends upon these interrelations with the context because individually and collectively they regulate and control its *resources*. The head is not the only person who handles all these relations, but they set the example on which the regulation and control will be exercised by others.

Implications III
Mobilizing the context in support of the school

Leadership III
The quality of the headteacher's interactions with the context attracts senior leaders of businesses and the professions to become school governors, and wins the support of parents. This mobilizes Positive Projected Power (P+p) in the interests of the school. The school's reputation in the local community opens up possibilities for joint projects with businesses. There may be a downside where poor school performance and bad behaviour amongst pupils and teachers may conflict with the hard work put into public relations by the head, which results in loss of confidence in the school and Negative Projected Power (P-P). This challenges the head to work to transform this negative situation into a positive one. The more they can raise wider awareness of the real purpose of the school, the more they can work through the negativity, seeking to grasp its meaning and creatively mobilize the energy in the interests of the school.

Management III
All these engagements with other systems and institutions require sophisticated managerial skill to implement their advantages in the life and work of the school. To emphasize the importance of the need for space to consider the implications of these interactions between the school and its context, the system diagram (Diagram 9) can be elaborated by inserting another line enclosing the system (or subsystem) to form a double boundary. This double boundary represents the opportunity to monitor and regulate the decisions being made by the headteacher (and where appropriate the Senior Leadership Team) about the inputs to and the outputs from the system in accordance with its aim. The diagram illustrating the personal managing boundary (Diagram 5) is extended here, applying the same principle of a 'skin' or boundary to the idea of a system, relating its in-

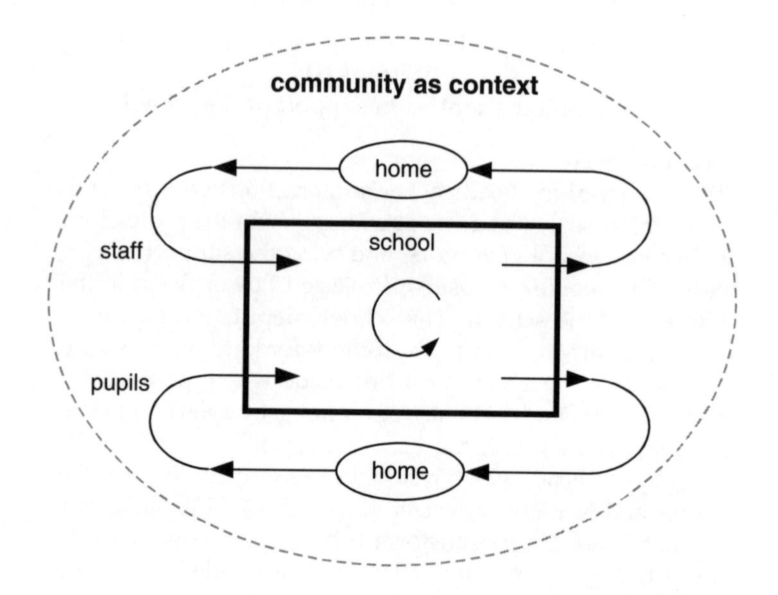

Figure 9: The school interacting with its context.

ner world of activities, persons, intentions, resources and so on to its outer contexts of other people, communities, institutions *etc*. To achieve this, the head needs to locate themselves on the boundary of the school, not at its centre (Official Power), drawing attention to all the other subsystem boundaries from which other people in the school operate, including the pupils.

This systems model counteracts the propensity of so many leaders and managers to locate themselves at the 'centre of things', e.g. the centre of the oblong which represents the system. We have in the past called the model of the head who tries to function entirely as if they were at the centre of everything the *'tribal chief'* model. What Diagram 10 shows is management on the boundary, in the margin between the inside and the outside

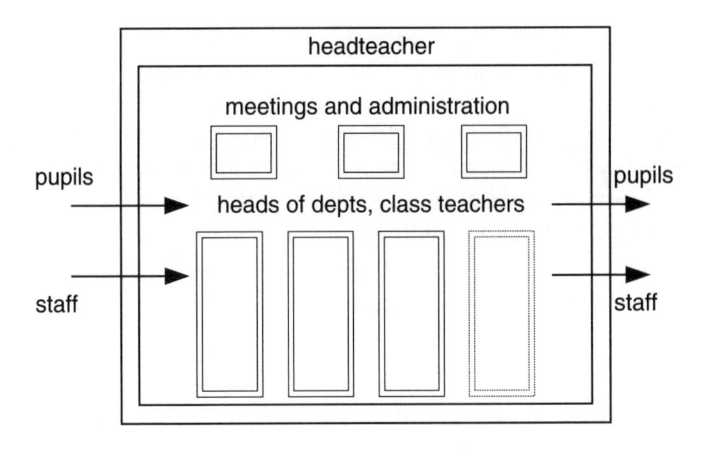

Figure 10: The school as a system with operating and service systems.

of the system. The space between the lines indicates the pause for reflection before decisions are made, and gives time for regulation of the forces injected by inputs, and for considering how the system can maximize their benefit – all these are indicators as to how management functions effectively. This systems conception is essential if any model of management at other levels is to be implemented with a sense of real freedom and authority.

Jill Clough comments: A head needs to guard against devoting too much time to getting goodwill from outside bodies rather than getting it from parents. This is especially true in terms of getting Positive Projections (P+p) from those parents who did not choose to send their children to your school. Losing the trust of parents leads to a very dangerous situation for the school.

Heads who work on the boundary of their school, rather than at its 'centre', and encourage their colleagues to do so too can sometimes find themselves criticized by advisers and inspectors who work with another model of management and who do not see the need for all the work of the school to be contextualized. This raises important questions about what we mean by 'school' so we are back to 'school-in-the-mind' and how the boundary is conceptualized as not simply being a physical thing.

Role

We have already begun to describe how we think about role, but it is now time to take that thinking further. As we said earlier, the headteacher's experience of his/her behaviour in *role* represents a shift away from the usual concept of role which is seen in concrete terms, as if it were a thing, rather than an idea in the mind that influences behaviour. If it is seen as an entity, role becomes something people can delegate, people can be appointed to a role and it can be described objectively, e.g. a role specification.

However, the interesting thing about human beings behaving is that they find that they cannot conform slavishly to job descriptions without feeling they are being turned into automatons. Persons respond to the fluid realities that confront them; they make judgements and modify their behaviour in ways that any job description could not predict. By contrast, we assume a role is an *idea-in-the-mind* which a person appointed to a position or delegated to a task needs to discover and develop in order to act in the best interests of the system.

We often use the analogy of a skilful small-boat sailor to help envisage what it means to take a role. To achieve the mark the sailor is alert to a whole range of dynamic factors: wind direction, currents, and the boat's special handling characteristics in relation to wind and water. The sailor is constantly trimming the helm, calculating where the mark is, perhaps tacking back and forth to sail against the wind if it is unfavourable. Just as the sailor 'disciplines' himself and his boat, taking a role, is how a person disciplines their own behaviour to carry out the aim of the system, by relating their interpretation of who and where they are, and how they experience the dynamics, the problems and the uncertainties of the system. It is worth remembering that, in the end, my own behaviour is the behaviour over which I have greatest control.

We call this process *working in role,* which is the outcome of the three conscious phases of activity described earlier: (a) finding the role (b) making the role and (c) taking the role. As we pointed out then, these phases overlap and reinforce each other, so when taking the role, the person goes deeper into finding the role, which develops the making and strengthens the taking of the role. Role is dynamic as the person working in role responds as the circumstances in the context change, the state of the relations in the system between persons and groups develop or deteriorate, and the policies of the system are altered.

This internal discipline *results in changed behaviour* on the role-taker's part, but it has implications for others who relate to them in that role. Other people do not 'see' a role, what they see and experience is the behaviour of the role-taker. They may interpret the situation differently, they may disagree with the actions of the role-taker, making the assumption that their expectation of his/her behaviour ought to be different. This may or may not be true and only by testing such behaviour with fresh evidence of what is happening in the system in relation to its aim can another role-taker decide which is the better judgement. Technically, the mental construct of the role-taker can be called, the *psychological role,* and the mental picture of others who see the behaviour, the *sociological role.*

Some headteachers instinctively work in role without knowing or appreciating the details of the process. However, when going into a new school, facing radical changes in the school, or under pressure of work, heads can lose their sense of role. If they react by behaving personally to defend themselves (*Experiential Power – Px*), they deflect their energies from achieving the task of the system. They lose the plot, which is another way of saying that they have become de-skilled.

The benefit of working in role is not only that the headteachers can be more effective in the school, but their leadership encourages and enables others to learn to work in their roles. They exercise authority which others experience as giving them freedom to work, taking their own authority in their roles, as distinct from only using power (*Px*) which will constrain and suppress personalities and distract from the shared sense of purpose that can hold the whole system together with a sense of shared fulfilment.

Where headteachers have a body of religious belief that they draw on, influencing their behaviour, they are not working simply from something which is their own creation. Their *praxis* (the expression of their belief/theory in their practice) can be scrutinized against criteria which are available to everyone, via scripture or in other forms. A Jewish head would no doubt say the same, recalling God's promise to Abraham. It was evident that these Christian headteachers were not just working instinctively in role. For them to work in role was their response to God's calling (vocation) to be (head)teachers. As Christians, they had sensed God's call within themselves and in responding they received from God the wisdom and guidance to interpret God's purpose for their school and, through Jesus Christ, to receive the strength to achieve it. Their sense of vocation is being called to do something that is beyond their own interest. We quoted Henry Nouwen earlier saying that a Christian leader is responding to a promise which has been given them by God. It is this which explains why the three heads in the project were 'working in role' without realizing it. Like Moliere's M. Jourdain, they were speaking 'prose' all the time without knowing it. Others with other beliefs, which may be political or religious, may refer to their sense of social conscience. Some heads work with an amalgam of principles from Christianity, Buddhism and other beliefs.

In this respect, those who draw on one or other of the three Abrahamic religions share a sense of accountability to an Other who they believe is not just their own personal construction. The end test is the extent to which the head's belief enables him or her to know how to find, make and take their role. It will be clear to their pupils, staff, governors and parents how far their belief is authentic and thus worth emulating.

Implications IV
Expressing one's beliefs in one's visible practice

Leadership IV
The test of the head's leadership is their *praxis*,[13] which is the expression through behaviour of their principles, theories and faith. Through this integration, they open the way for their staff and their pupils to follow them if they wish to do so. At least they have the freedom to do it. Christian headteachers find, make and take their leadership role in the school, realizing their own limitations. As one head said when asked what happens if they succeed in transforming the school, *'I will give God all the credit.'* Here we encounter *Spiritual Power (Ps).* This is why the head's belief cannot be a private matter nor is it simply a matter of 'life-style'. Those with deep religious beliefs can do no other than embody them in their actions, which are open to scrutiny by all, who judge not only the person, but the beliefs expressed in their *praxis*. Their integrity is most evident when they can use the language which articulates their faith, linking it to the way they work as head and to the ways in which they relate to children and adults connected with the school. This is not conventional 'evangelism', but a way of speaking wisely about Reality.

Management IV
Management converts the vision generated in leadership to reality through the consistency of the decisions and determinations. In decision making and deploying their school's resources, the head is prepared to take risks in making the school fit for its purpose. Things which are fit for purpose are not necessarily flawless – a cracked jug can pour water effectively. The head's found, made and taken management role is continually adapting to internal and external pressures, as all the time the head is seeking to establish a cli-

mate in the school where people feel liberated, free to use their imagination, able to be open with one another and everyone knows how to belong.

Jill Clough comments: In a faith based school, children, staff and parents respond with relief when the head can declare, 'This is what I believe and that lies behind what I say and do.' This enables others to gain a measure of how to relate to you and work with you. Problems arise if people are unable to see where you are coming from; your behaviour is open to being interpreted as ambiguous, leading to distrust and cynicism.

Spelling out the headteacher's experience of behaviour in role is at the core of the Venn diagram (Diagram 2). It constitutes the head's contribution to the whole school curriculum, where the 'curriculum' is understood not simply as the planned and taught material, but the lived experience of being a member of the school. This involves the head in converting national policies, LEA guidance, governors' decisions, parents' wishes, teachers' skills and ideas, and children's capabilities into a workable, resilient and relevant system of activities; not only this, they demonstrate that as managers they accept full accountability for how these are all integrated day by day in what children and adults experience in the school.

3.3 The Christian head's leadership in transformative behaviour

Before going on to look at the headship of community schools in the next chapter, we will summarize our findings about the three Church of England schools with Christian headteachers. We will indicate that the acknowledged transformation of their schools was more than the result of the headteachers' professional competence and energy. The 'plus factor' we were researching was that the personal belief of these Christian headteachers was that pupils and staff could change their behaviour; and this belief was based on their own experience of transformation through Christ. Their skill in relating to pupils, staff, parents and significant authorities enabled them to express their convictions wisely, not only in words, but through the organization and management of their schools which resulted in improved personal and organizational performance by everyone who belonged to the school.

Inclusiveness: the Church of England school's unique gift to British society

A major obstacle that needs to be overcome when thinking about church schools is the accusation that church schools exist to evangelize and recruit members to its ranks, feeding prejudice and division in society. It is true that there are Anglican schools that run exclusive intake policies, fostering cynical church attendance in order to win places in them, providing a covert process of selection of more 'desirable' children to the school. There are also well-publicized schools which teach syllabuses that are at odds with the curriculum taught in most other schools. However, this was emphatically not true of these three schools. These were community schools in the full sense of being led and managed in ways intended to provide education for any children that came to them from their local community, whatever their nationality, creed or ability.

They fulfilled the intention in the Dearing Report on the Church of England's schools:

> *The Church's approach to education as a whole ... is one founded on a notion of inclusiveness rather than separation from the community. ... The composition of its school population ... will reflect the composition of the neighbourhood and must therefore be inclusive of all ethnicity, belief and social class.*[14]

The headteachers' skills in interpersonal relations, group relations and institutional relations were sharpened by their belief and love for their pupils, their clarity about the purpose of their school in its community context and their ability to work in role to behave with authority. The school became a facilitating learning environment in which everyone could have freedom, scope and incentive to grow and develop.

The diversity of the Christian backgrounds of the three heads showed they were not following some previously known and trodden paths. Two Roman Catholics and one Free Church member working in Church of England schools had to innovate and plan their work on the spot with the assistance of clergy, teachers and officials from the Church of England. The experience of three non-Anglicans was that these Church of England schools were open to them. It was therefore logical that they would grasp the principle of *inclusion* as the basis for relations to pupils coming from other faiths, expressing it in their leadership of their schools. They knew tensions would arise naturally within the school organization, but they knew they could place the matter in the widest context of God's love and care for every human being, believing they could manage any difficulties which arose.

Being a 'living God' implies a God living with his world, his creation and his people. Theologically, we believe in God as *transcendent*, above and beyond human understanding, before and beyond all worlds, and who is also *immanent*, among us and engaging with us humans in all aspects of our lives.

The headteacher who is Christian is open to spelling out the question: *How is God present? What is God doing in the day-to-day life of the school?* If the nature of God's activity, the *opus Dei*, can be discerned, then we believe the Christian head's response will be to behave in harmony with that activity as it is interpreted in a specific situation at the time. This involves working with reality, however good or bad and whatever the effects may be.

From our reading of Scripture, there are three major reference points in Christian theology about God's activity: God as *creator*, God as *redeemer and sustainer*, God as *king and judge*. The Bible indicates points on the time/space continuum for each of these activities, the creator at the beginning; the redeemer in Jesus' death; and the king at the end; but all three are confirming acts of God throughout 'time', always creating new and anew, always redeeming and saving, and always ruling as king and judge.

These three aspects of God's living presence among us are points of reference for locating the limitless variations of God's relations with his world, beyond our comprehension. Among us God works continuously – dramatically, slowly, consciously and unconsciously. The presences of God in Christian theology, are attributed to members of the Holy Trinity, Father, Son and Holy Spirit. Where One is, there are the Others. Christians associate the Father with transcendence, the Son with all that is created, redeemed and judged, and the Holy Spirit with indwelling presence in sustaining that creation.

The sensitive Christian head, by interpreting what is happening in the various aspects of school life, can discern and interpret how God is present. Herein lies the deepest wisdom available to them. The head's response to this situation is to mirror those actions of God in dealing with pupils, staff, parents, governors *etc*, believing that God's guidance will lead to just outcomes.

The whole school curriculum can be interpreted as co-operating with God as *creator* in developing imagination, skills and fresh understandings, setting up the school in the community with its building and technologies with human and other resources. The potential understanding of creativity comes through the study of all subjects, but especially in poetry, music, arts, dance, mathematics and the sciences, expanding and deepening pupils' perceptions of God's world of which they are living and active parts.

Building up working relations with concern and love for all in the school, especially the weak and resistant, reveals God's own initiative in *redemption* as open to all to receive his forgiveness: staff expressing their care for pupils despite mistakes and blunders, and similarly for colleagues and on some occasions deliberately destructive acts, is evidence of God's redemptive work. As one pupil said about his headteacher, *'she never gives up on you'*. The reality of forgiveness through Christ's work in us transforms difficult relationships.

Whenever staff and pupils exercise authority and acknowledge their accountability for the standards of their work and behaviour, God is working in and alongside them as *king and judge*. God is not a 'soft touch' but One who is truth and reality. Ofsted inspections that draw attention to poor teaching, bad management and failures to serve the interests of children's education are manifestations of God's work as judge. These are realities that the three heads in the study recognized as framing the challenge before them and the reality with which they must deal. They accepted Jesus Christ who said, *'I am the way that leads to the reality of life'*, [St John's Gospel: 14.6]. For them the 'reality of life' is a life skilfully lived in all its fullness, not in a state of slavery or subjugation to other persons, ideologies, drugs or addictions.

At every level, God is active and open to the response of each person in carrying out his purpose for their lives. Most pupils and staff may not be aware of these acts of God's grace. The skill of the Christian headteacher is, through example, to allow everyone the space to discover the richness of the possibilities to all, whoever they are and wherever they come from.

This line of interpretation models the school as part of the Kingdom of God rather than as the 'Church'. The task of the Church is to serve this Kingdom. Jesus' teaching in the Gospels was about the Kingdom, with himself as the king, which transcends religion whether Jew, Christian, Muslim, Hindu, Sikh *etc.* The prayer Jesus taught his disciples was to pray for the Kingdom, where the petition reflects the three reference points: *give us this day our daily bread* – creator; *forgive us our sins as we forgive those who sin against us* – redeemer; *and deliver us from evil* – king and judge. We pray for the Kingdom which is present – *the Kingdom is yours,* and yet is coming – *your Kingdom come.*

Experiences in school that run along these lines provide a basis for understanding some of the deepest undercurrents in British life, which seldom surface in clear forms. This country has a history that is steeped in Christian understanding.

The country's policy towards convicted offenders who are sent to prison is a current arena where whether national policy on sentencing is for punishment, rehabilitation or redemption is not clear. Experience in school of the possibility to repent and change can frame thinking and behaviour for a lifetime. To go further, in the legal system, ethical questions such as those currently posed by stem-cell research wrestle with understandings about human life and the relatedness of one human being with others. Any one of today's school children may be faced with having to make choices about having a family or the cure of an illness: they need some basis for thinking through the decision they will make and the law will influence what they do.

Jill Clough comments: The head of a school with a faith base is challenged to live out the belief they claim. They need to behave 'as if' these things were true and to discover through faith whether they are or not. This is not a case of polemics, but of life in action. This is seldom more true than in the case of valuing children's talent. If you believe that each person, whatever age, is made in the image of God, you carry a duty to value all pupils, not just some. Pupils will know the value you put on them, even if you are not personally aware of them individually.

Becoming fit for the Kingdom: the significance of worship in school life

Worship in a Church of England school is the Church at prayer for the school as Kingdom, which is the culmination of all the teaching and learning by pupils and staff in the school, responding to the *opus Dei*. Inclusion of other beliefs is not an option, but a condition of being the Kingdom of Christ, which challenges Christian theology at its deepest. The Jews in Jesus' time could not see the possibilities of the Kingdom in their time, can we Christians see it today?

Implications V
Leading the Church school's fullest purpose

Leadership V
Leadership of any school for a Christian headteacher is a spiritual task, since God's activity is there, whether or not it is being consciously experienced by head, staff and pupils. In a Church of England school where God is worshipped openly, the headteacher is given the opportunity to acknowledge God's rule. To demonstrate the corporate spiritual process of the school by reflecting in that leadership the different ways God relates to the school and its members. God invites them to achieve his purpose for their lives – children in their emerging adulthood, adults in their careers and vocations, to realize the vision of becoming fit for his Kingdom.

Management V
The shortfall of resources can swamp managers with anxiety which blurs their vision for the purpose of the school. The Christian headteacher can draw on God's resources to contain those anxieties within him/herself so that they do not undermine the effort of others. The headteacher can learn to deploy what resources there are with hope and encouragement, because the vision is not one of a perfect school, but one that becomes fit for purpose.

3.4 Leading assembly & worship in community schools

At the end of section 2.2 where we explored things said to us about the life of three church schools, we described what pupils, teachers, heads and others said about worship in those schools. Over the years, we have explored in our other work, the place of religion in society and in a range of different institutions. We have worked on the assumption – originally put forward by the Tavistock psychoanalyst Wilfred Bion – that every gathering of human beings, especially in formal institutions, develops a 'religion'. By this he drew on the root of the Latin word *religare,* which means 'to bind' and he went further to include what the *New Oxford Dictionary of English* refers to as 'obligation, bond and reverence'. No human enterprise can be effective without these factors, and schools need formal ways of incorporating them into their routines so that children learn about them in preparation for adult life.

This section explores the significance of assembly as the event that provides the foundation of the effective life of the school and what holds the school together. Assembly is the place where all the other diverse bits of the school can be brought together so that the whole can make sense. In a Church school, the 'making sense' can use the Christian faith to go beyond the internal life of the school and to look out across society and the world. In another school sponsored by another faith the same can happen. In each community school, the head has to find some basis on which to open up the internal life of the school to that wider context. For some, this might be a political belief or a deeply held philosophy. What is important is that *being* the head means that each headteacher is tested personally in this respect and the effectiveness of their school depends on how they respond.

A theory of religion in society

The heart of the approach we have taken is spelled out in Bruce Reed's book *The Dynamics of Religion*[15] which described his Oscillation theory of religion in society in the culture of the United Kingdom. He opened the issue out so as to develop a Christian point of view, but the argument is, in the first place, a human one. Work has been done on the application of Reed's theory to schools. He applied it in a particularly illuminating way to the function of worship in chapel in independent schools. This was outlined in a paper delivered to the Bloxham Conference of

1981 and published in the Bloxham Project Newsletter of Summer 1981 which provides the background to what we have to say about principles of school leadership through worship in this section.[16]

The 1944 Education Act has undergone many changes and amendments, but one part has continued to be legally in effect. This is that every school should have a daily act of collective worship of a broadly Christian kind. Though this clause is closer than ever to being dropped, it is remarkable that it has continued for so long. One key question that any government re-examining this provision will be bound to ask is, *'What underlying wisdom is there which, despite our national cultural and religious changes since 1944, still holds good today?'* What these three schools suggest is that there is a human factor that any reforming government would be unwise to ignore. We would not want to invite schools simply to conform with the law because it is there: that is a recipe for providing an example of compliance and hypocrisy rather than professional accountability and maturity. However, the psychological and emotional contribution of coming together for assembly can be understood in terms of the healthy functioning of the school. In this way, assembly can become part of the *maturational* process of the school, not an imposed ritual which reinforces unthinking compliance, hampering healthy growing up.

'Religion' in institutions

All human institutions contain within them a range of feelings, only some of which match one another and many of which are in tension. Feelings of joy, excitement, satisfaction and fulfilment exist alongside, fear, uncertainty, anger and frustration; together, these make up the reality of the life of the institution. Many feelings are stimulated by things that are real in the outside world, but many spring from images and dreams which, though not based on fact, are still real factors in the life of the institution. This mixture of feelings and fantasies lurking under the surface of the institution's life, provides the ingredients for chaos which might erupt at any moment, producing disorder and danger for people trying to work together. So as not to be emotionally disabled, groups evolve rituals to tidy up and contain this risky brew, often without any conscious planning. These practices have been called the 'group ethos', to which everyone in the institution becomes subject and often an unwitting participant.[17]

Addressing the fundamental questions about human life in society – birth, the education of the young, the creation and distribution of wealth, the cure of the sick and the care of the dying – raises all those feelings that can become the most powerful drivers towards chaos. In places of work dealing with these questions such as schools, hospitals, churches and so on, professional disciplines – teaching, psychology, medicine, theology and so on – shape the 'group ethos' by drawing on values, procedures, rules and rituals which can contain the potential chaos and, properly handled, can mobilize energy in support of the institution's purpose.

These factors combine to produce what has been called 'civil religion'. This is specific to each institution, helping that institution to contain and control the way people live and function together within it. The 'religion' sustained by persons and artefacts, especially by those who symbolize it most clearly, for example in a hospital, the wearing of white coats, uniforms and suits expresses the hierarchy of those working there. Actively and passively, these different persons heighten the institution's awareness of certain things, whilst shading out awareness of others. The artefacts include parts of the building, portraits, mottos, equipment, notices, honours boards and so on. Though it does not rely on any overt reference to a deity, the institution's religion nevertheless endows these persons and artefacts with an aura of sacredness.

'Religion' in schools

In 1979 Michael Rutter pointed out that *'pupils are subject to a group influence resulting from the ethos of the school'*.[18] This ethos is powerful and unless the school leadership and management take its existence into account in how the school goes about its daily life, the underlying possibility for chaos can break loose; even 'mild' outbreaks affect the work of the school and the capacity of pupils and staff to work effectively in achieving the school's purpose. A continuous failure over time to contain the potential chaos creates a vicious circle from which a school may never recover.

The civil religion of a school includes some of the following functions: celebrating the school's values; enabling pupils to think well of their school; linking the school's past – its former students and its past achievements – to the present; making pupils aware of their responsibility for the present quality of life in the school; reminding them of the values, principles and beliefs that make the school what it is, the stories and myths through which those principles and beliefs are passed on, making the intangible ethos more accessible. School uniform has an important part to play in this.

There are five key functions of the school's 'civil religion' and its rituals, in particular assembly:

1. By focusing and controlling the covert chaos and containing the anxiety present in the school, all the school's members can get on with the school's overt agenda of teaching and learning in classrooms.

2. Since everyone participates in the school's ethos (not necessarily positively, but to react against it is to take part in making it what it is) the school feels itself to be a 'whole' and living body.

3. The religion permeates the political structure of the school which formally bonds everyone in it together. At an obvious level, this bonding is helped by consistent wearing of the school uniform by pupils; but the adults are also part of the institution.

4. Staff participation provides a covert message about the kind of inclusion and exclusion that their school has. One

factor in this is that, given the unconscious processes that take place in large groups, the mythical dimension of the school touches those who take part in worship with a sense of the sacredness of the school. In a school we worked in some years ago, the children consistently described the place as a 'prison'. Observing an assembly, we saw all the students sitting on the floor while the women teachers – all in black fashion boots – patrolled around them issuing sharp rebukes. The unconscious modelling picked by the boys and girls was obvious.

5. Because it is a 'religion' in the strict sense of the term, conscious and unconscious drives will seek some clear symbol of the unity of whole: the natural figure to whom this task is offered is the headteacher. This calls upon the head to be the symbol of everything that the school stands for, whatever their personal beliefs. As one pupil put it in the church schools study: *'Yes, I do think that students do make an effort because of the head. He motivates us during assemblies and gives us an insight on what he is intending to do.'*

A civil religion in a school is not intended to challenge the school's values and ethos, though it is expected to uphold them, to make them intelligible and acceptable to all its members. These values may or may not correlate closely with values experienced by pupils at home and in the local community. If a school's 'religion' is at odds with the values of the world outside, work needs to be done to convince people that the school's values are actually those of the much wider world. If they can be internalized, they can help to move beyond the restrictions of the school's immediate local setting. If the school fails to do this, students who move between the school's world and the local context may find themselves faced with unmanageable tensions between home and school which will in due course be acted out in one place or the other, or even in both.

To the extent that the head and senior staff grasp the significance of the school's civil religion and work with it, an internal culture can be fostered which can include all the personal belief systems of its members, including those of Christians, Jews, Moslems, Hindus, Sikhs, agnostics and atheists. Central to grasping this is the question of being clear about what will advance the school's well-being, uniting all its members.

That is a key task of headship.

Civil religion in community schools: its relatedness to Christian faith

What the wise Christian headteacher in a community school does is to see the shortcoming of civil religion alone for the fullness of the task ahead of them. The subtlety of civil religion is that it can apparently be 'Christian' because it may use 'Christian' words and scriptural references. This is also true in church schools where the transforming impact of the experience of the person of Jesus Christ is lacking.

Wise Christian heads explore and test the kinds of motivation that underpin the way anyone conducts worship, including themselves. The question to be asked is, *'Does the way the Gospel is presented here create opportunities for the transformation of persons and of the school as a whole?'* Where civil religion confirms the school's values, the Gospel actually subjects even the school's 'good' values to question and scrutiny, placing them under judgement. On important occasions, the Gospel may actually attack the whole existing ethos of the school but do that by raising realistic ways to move forward from the present state of affairs.

Jill Clough comments: In a school where the head sets out to contain and 'hold' the whole school through acts of worship, what you do needs to be done with conviction. You need to act from the heart. When you do not – and no-one can do it all the time day in day out through the whole school year – that will be recognized by all those present. If you have laid down a basis of trust in your integrity, then you falling short will be understood and forgiven.

Where the school's coming together is in worship, rather than a 'school assembly', those who gather together can feel that it is proper to bring with them their doubts, weaknesses, despair, vulnerability and all their assumptions about themselves and others. They can then subject them to the scrutiny of God who is Himself at one and the same time transcendent and suffering, powerful and vulnerable, remote and pervasive. The way the worship is conducted creates moods of awe, joy, peace, anger, love and justice which evoke within the worshippers the authentic parts of themselves, allowing them to feel *real*. At moments, those values which one takes for granted can be shown up quite differently in the light of God's truth. As a result, the person can go forth from the assembly with a heightened sense of their power to question what has hitherto been tacitly approved. This capacity to question oneself and others in radical ways is the basis of true transformation.

The experience of God manifested through occasions like these, opens up the opportunity for an image of God to emerge that is not simply a school deity, created out of a mosaic of the school's values (particularly probably the head's) but someone truly Other. From the encounter with that Other, each person can engage in a different kind of self-understanding while discovering that in this school one has the freedom to be oneself. In this way, other approaches to religious belief are neither ruled out, nor accepted without thought.

The fundamental task of school assembly in this sense is to enable everyone who participates in it to leave that gathering, unencumbered by the burdens they took into it and ready to tackle the challenges of the practicalities of engaging with other pupils and teachers in the daily work in the classroom, laboratory, gym and playground. As one headteacher in the study put it when describing how his senior staff thought about worship in their school:

We try to create young people who have a mind-set about themselves and the institution so that they can become learners. If you've got pupils who feel positive about themselves and about learning they can go to class to be partners with the teachers.

Authors' Comment: This way of understanding worship in society and institutions is developed by Bruce Reed in his Oscillation Theory of religion. This theory postulates that human life is lived in a constant process, as natural as breathing, between a mode of behaviour in which one engages with the practical world of the tasks and work that sustain life and a mode in which one is aware of doubts, despair, vulnerability and the need for something or someone secure on which to depend. In communities and societies, religious institutions – churches, synagogues, mosques, ghudwaras and temples – carry this out for members of that community. In a school, this natural process can be harnessed through the structuring of the life of the school. The theory is fully described and extended in Reed's book *The Dynamics of Religion* (op.cit).

Such a combination of the school's civil religion with the Christian faith has major implications for the headteacher. Each head has to accept that the other human beings connected with the school will inevitably use the head's role as a focus for their own need for psychological survival and security. *There is no choice about being the head of the civil religion,* but a wise Christian head will be prepared to become this figure upon whom the whole body of persons depend, being ready to analyze the range of feelings projected into them – of power and weakness, beauty and beastliness, doubt and certainty, neediness and fulfilment. Much of this they can only be partially aware of and some of it they can never fulfil: yet they find the courage and strength to go on. As one head in the study put it:

What I have sought to develop here is the ability to be yourself and to be vulnerable ... Admit your mistakes, we're all beggars helping each other to find bread ... My experience is of my own Christian salvation. I am in need of forgiveness and I've found the person who forgives me; so I have nothing to fear; I have no fear of failure.

Though that head may not fear failure, this was no excuse for being insouciant. Opportunities for self-examination occur during worship, in particular about how one has used one's powers as head teacher – experiential (*Px*), official (*Po*), instrumental (*Pi*), projected (*Pp*) and spiritual (*Ps*) power. Testing their use of those powers against the purpose of the school reveals the extent to which power has been used to energize the authority of their headship. The test each head can apply is to observe how far others in every role in the school are learning to take their own authority, to find, make and take their own roles, so that together they can further what the school is for.

Chapter 4

Implications

In this chapter we will open up the question of pupil leadership. This is not simply about the head's leadership of the pupils, which is important enough, but about how pupils can be equipped so that their resources can be released for the transformation of the school. We will describe how pupils can be fully engaged in the transformation of their schools and we will discuss what needs to be done to prepare teachers to respond creatively to leadership from pupils.

So what does it mean for a school to become fit for purpose? The obvious answer is that it is a school that equips its students to engage with the adult world, to be able to take responsibility for themselves, their families, their workplace and for their community. Schools deemed by Ofsted inspectors to be failing to do that are placed in Special Measures and have to work dedicatedly to improve what they are doing. At the beginning of this book the question was posed: 'What do Christian headteachers who transform church schools actually do?' Of course, a sample of three is not enough to answer the question with complete certainty.

However, what these three have been doing may ring bells with other headteachers wishing to emulate them, for them either to feel that they can now see more clearly the significance of things they have done instinctively, or to adopt similar practices to the ones these three have used. There are enough aspects described here of what they did, for heads of other faiths or none to consider what they do and to find here things that resonate for them too.

There are five issues to be drawn out.

1. ***Enabling children to belong to the school***
   The students in these schools demonstrated that all three heads had enabled them to feel they belonged. There is a saying: in European culture *'I think, therefore I am'* (or feel real); in African culture *'I belong, therefore I am'* (or feel real). These heads enabled their students to feel real. Because they felt real they could work and play more effectively and therefore feel more fulfilled. They did this because they knew how to find, make and take the pupil role in the school. Enabling the adults – teachers, support staff and governors – also came to feel that they belonged to the school: it was more than just a place of work to them.

   Jan Carlson, the very successful chief executive of the airline SAS, told the story of two men working a quarry. One was sullen, bad tempered and careless; the other was alert, imaginative and a true craftsman. When asked what they were doing the former replied 'I'm doing this because I have to earn a living'; the latter replied 'I am helping to build the cathedral'.

2. ***Feeling mutually accountable***
   The heads worked in ways that developed a culture of mutual accountability between everyone in the school. The heads themselves, the teaching staff, the support staff, the pupils, their parents and the governors felt that what they did had implications for everyone else and thus for the school as a whole. To put this in terms of roles, because the heads found, made and took their roles in ways that everyone else could understand, other roles could be found, made and taken in compatible ways. Thus, everyone becomes mutually accountable for the school and, since good

schools are generators of healthy local communities, mutually accountable for what the school does to contribute to the well-being of its local community and so to society as a whole.

3. ***Mobilizing the natural processes of human interaction and development appropriately***
By creating structures that enabled the four processes in the Reed Rainbow – belonging, learning, empowering and transforming – to be separated and focused, the specialist work in subject classes, tutoring and school assembly could be done without cluttering each other up. A synergy between what everyone did was then possible.

4. ***Gaining the confidence of agencies outside the school***
Schools that succeed do so at least as much as a result of the emotional and other support they can gain from those in the school's context. The heads drew actively on imaginative support from such bodies as the Diocese, the local education authority, the local press and media.

5. ***Making worship a central activity of the school***
All three heads took worship as an activity. It underpinned the school and its purpose, making it a place that people felt was worth belonging to, but which also challenged itself in areas where things might be taken for granted and self-satisfaction might creep in.

Each of these has been described and explored in what has gone before. It is time to focus on what these heads and others who find themselves in sympathy with them might do to take things further. The question is not about making a long list of recommendations, but focusing on the most critical things to take into account; there are three of these:

1. Pupil leadership and school transformation.

2. Attending to the formation of wise heads.

3. Church of England schools being inclusive.

which we consider in the following sections.

4.1 Pupil leadership and school transformation

Leadership of the pupils

Those who have most to gain – and lose – from their school being either successful or in difficulties are the children themselves. Heads and teachers can move on; governors can resign; local authorities can close a school down, while locally elected members and officers continue on their ways; but the children have only those years in school, after which they must face the adult world in whatever condition they may be. As one head we quoted put it: *'My motivation is my belief that the children only have one chance.'*

In all these three schools the heads mobilized the pupils to take their part in transforming their school. A pupil in one school has been quoted saying: *'I do think that students make an effort because of the Head. He motivates us during assemblies and gives us an insight on what he is intending to do.'* He did not see that this was simply about getting better SATs and GCSE results, but about changing the whole of the school culture. This is an example of the head paying attention to leading the pupils.

Belonging, learning, empowering and transforming

Evidence given earlier was that the heads all established a working relation between themselves in role and the children in their role as pupils and learners. Quotation after quotation underlined this from pupils themselves, teachers, parents, governors and heads. Pupils began to believe in themselves, they began to respond and to discover that the school was there for them: each one of them might have been able to say *'all of this is for me'*.

New pupils could begin their life in the school on the basis of believing that they belonged. The point is that *belonging* is fundamental since it provides the secure basis for education and learning in the classroom as well as more widely. Conventional success academically is the result, perhaps not immediately, but cumulatively over time.

Classroom *learning* contributes to the process of growing up to a certain degree, but necessarily tends to focus less on the individual person's growth and development. Learning in the wider sense, including learning to take up roles that influence the wider institution, calls for work at a different dimension of experience. There are two points to be made about this.

1. First of all, one needs greater maturity and greater power to work at this dimension. Learning to study an academic subject effectively does involve self-discipline of one kind, but being responsible for aspects of school life, some of which may include challenging others who are also one's friends, is new and different.

2. Being able to develop a wider vision – of oneself, of what might be achieved if one put one's mind to it – opens up the possibility of *personal transformation* and of *organizational transformation* as well. And this is not just about being consulted – though that is a start.

There are two sides to belonging: when one says, 'I belong to ... my family, my school, my nation ...', one places oneself within that system. A prisoner when asked in which prison he belongs might reply, 'I belong in Pentonville Prison'. Many children might feel the same about their school.

But we also say, 'This belongs to me. This is *my* family, this is *my* school, this is *my* nation ...' This is about ownership. The evidence was that pupils learned to feel that the school belonged to them; they liked the way outsiders spoke about it, gaining kudos and expressing pride in it. They recognized that they were contributors to the school's reputation and could own it. To be able to do this calls for a different kind of learning which raises new questions.

The school's successes and failures are not just about exam performance or sports contests won, though those are important and the person's part in those results gives pleasure and satisfaction. But things do not always go well, so the school can also be a source of despair and anger. Owning the school's ethos includes owning the respect accorded to its members, the ways in which resistance and opposition are dealt with. Coming to own the negative as well as the positive dimensions of institutional life, provides major opportunities for personal learning. In fact, this learning is in practice fundamental to building a healthy democratic society.

Jill Clough comments: For most children being able to take the step of owning the negative about the school may be one step too far. However, it may be worth aiming as high as possible to discover what can be achieved by some children.

To be able to take ownership of both the good and the bad – in oneself and even more difficult in a system as a whole – is a matter of *empowerment*. It calls for maturity of a kind that does not just happen, but needs to be fostered and developed, both by the person and by others who create opportunities for it to take place.

Leadership by the pupils

Heads can open up the opportunity for children to mature by being empowered by finding ways of enabling the children to offer leadership to the school as a whole. This is, of course, what happens in the best models of prefect systems and school councils. But this can be taken further.

At the present moment, young people's participation in their schools and other institutions is a major area of government policy and is also a matter of major interest to others. At the 15th Conference of Commonwealth Education Ministers in October 2003, responding to the parallel Youth Summit – at which the young people said, *'We can't do it ourselves, but you can't do it without us'* – Commonwealth Ministers committed themselves to the maximum possible involvement of young people.

In principle, teachers welcome pupil participation. The myriad of websites on pupil participation and pupil leadership usually refer to school councils and prefect systems, resulting in levels of pupil influence on what happens in a school. Peer counselling, tackling bullying, pupil/pupil mediation, addressing behaviour and attendance are all referred to amongst the range of things being practised at the moment. Research from the Economic and Social Research Council confirms the importance of this kind of participation in enabling the growth of self-esteem, motivation, sense of ownership, improved attendance, enhanced attainment and empowerment.

There are steps which could be taken that open up the pupil's perspective on critical school matters that are faced by the leadership and management of the school, not simply as matters of opinion, but as soundly based realities upon which overall school development policy and the School Action Plan can be based. The Children's Research Centre at the Open University has demonstrated that children as young as 9 and 10 can identify real issues that concern them, undertake sound research and report objectively upon their findings to major adult bodies.

Pupils almost certainly have their own view about the impact of bad behaviour and poor attendance on their effectiveness in school: they might believe that an investigation is needed into the underlying dynamics of bad behaviour and poor attendance of their contemporaries, which could lead to presenting new ideas about how those might be tackled to the head and governors. Given what we now know, can the pupil leadership be turbo-charged?

Preparing teachers for leadership by pupils

However good one's intentions may be to involve pupils in the management and leadership of the school, resistance is inevitable in human institutions. Teachers are properly conscious of their responsibility to be teachers, communicating their subject and other specialisms to children. It can appear at first sight as if one were proposing to license children to say and do things that would undermine the authority of teachers to do their job. This could provoke resistance and needs to be taken seriously.

If not, nothing of substance can be achieved. What these resistances are and how to handle them is a potential area for research. What is important is to face up to is how far this resistance is based on an underestimation of children's abilities to think and act strategically.

4.2 The formation of wise heads

Being equipped to be the head of a school in which the pupils take a substantial part in the school's leadership on the lines outlined above calls for preparation of a particular kind.

We explored three groups of leadership principles in Chapter 3: leadership of persons, leadership of systems and leadership of worship. All three are rooted in the head's capacity to work with their own experience in role, through which they model to everyone else how they can in turn work in their roles and experience the freedom which comes from being part of something bigger than themselves, feeling that they are partners in ownership.

The heads who took part in the study could work intuitively and skilfully in ways that opened up these issues, but, as any Olympic athlete knows, there is no end to honing one's skill. We can therefore outline the kind of programme that might be offered to those wishing to become heads of schools where leadership is inclusive.

The following are key ingredients of such a programme:

- Learning to work with their day to day *experience*.
- Providing the *concepts* from social science and theology required to interpret and analyze their experience. By this means, the heads learn a *praxis* of integrating theory and practice in their work.
- Developing these skills calls for *time* and space to stand far enough back to reflect on and interpret experience. It is especially important to provide sufficient time and space to acknowledge their difficulties openly with other heads.

For any transformation and understanding of roles to be achieved, it is not enough to give presentations and initiate general discussion. The depth that is required will come from disciplined study of real situations in which heads are currently involved, to generate and test hypotheses about the meaning of that situation for their schools.

Jill Clough comments: The National College for School Leadership has included this kind of work in their New Visions programmes. Unfortunately, such reflective work is not as 'neat' and 'quick' as directly taught programmes. This makes it more expensive in time, though participants consistently rate this work as having the highest value for them. Despite this, the most recent plans of the College are to cut it from the new versions of the programme.

- Such a programme will be carried out in a series of *modules*, some of a single day, others of 2/3 days, backed up by individual work with a consultant on critical issues arising in the leadership and management of the school, spaced out over time.

- Variations on the above can be developed to include other members of the school: pupils, staff working in different areas of the school's management.

Development for Governors

Governing bodies have a critical responsibility first of all to appoint headteachers and then to work with them once in post. We have made several references to the importance of the headteacher being able to envisage the school as a functioning whole. The same is also true of the governors. Most governing bodies are at risk of being overwhelmed by detail, becoming unable to differentiate out the strategic from the mundane. Where they can develop a shared, internalized image of their school and what it is for in their community, in which they see the school as serving that community inclusively, they can support and guide their head.

4.3 Being inclusive: gift and challenge

Faith schools in general have been the focus of strongly held opinions that believe them to be divisive. Most opposition rejects the idea of faith schools in any form. However, there are interesting variations, pressing them to be inclusive. In May 2004, the BBC published the findings of a survey that 75% of the 25/34 year age group think that the government should force faith schools to take pupils of other faiths and no faith.[19] This view, while taking out the compulsion, is in line with the intentions of the Dearing Review Group for the Church of England. It also accords with our thinking about the opportunities to learn for pupils and their school's contribution to the health and well-being of its local community.

The *principle of inclusion* has the potential for contributing to radical change in Britain's national culture. The more the Church of England can have the courage to put into practice and to publicize at every opportunity that its education policy is inclusive, the more the need for local communities to be healthy and prosperous (in every sense) can be met. As a result, the present, potentially unhealthy situation, can be challenged where white 'Christians' (who constitute 74% of Britain's population) rate 'religion' at the bottom of their list of ten factors important to their identity while placing income, and social class higher.[20]

To state it precisely, the Church of England through its inclusion policy is open to fostering the interaction of the Christian faith with other faiths, facilitating the emergence of new cultural norms in UK society. As the culture in our society becomes more diverse, Church of England schools are in a position to monitor these changes as they occur. They can provide containers in which differences can be understood and worked with, and can retard or even prevent the growth of splits that spring from differences which result in division, prejudice and racism.

This is an application of Jesus Christ's sayings:

> *Whoever wants to save his life will lose it, but whoever loses his life for my sake and for the gospel's will save it.*
>
> **[St Mark's Gospel 8:35]**

> *Jesus took a child, sat him in front of them, and put his arm around him, 'whoever receives a child like this in my name' he said, 'receives me...'*
>
> **[St Mark's Gospel 9: 36, 37]**

The Church of England can uniquely do this through its schools. Being the Established Church opens up the Church of England to this sense of responsibility for all people in its domain; church schools carry this through by the inclusion principles and may 'lose their lives' and be submerged in the emerging culture. Yet living inclusively in this way opens up the possibility of discovering in experience what it means to consider what it means to be the 'new humanity' in which there is *'no longer Greek and Jew, circumcised and uncircumcised, barbarian, Scythian, slave and Free'*.[21]

Given that the nineteenth-century Church of England first blazed the trail of education for everyone, the twenty-first century opens up the opportunity to blaze the trail for the education needed in the nation's diverse society. Far from holding the nation back, its schools can provide the paradigm for truly inclusive education.

There is a further factor which is facilitated by leading a Church of England school and available to Christian headteachers (of whatever denomination) and perhaps not to others of other faiths and beliefs. As we have shown, the Christian head is interpreting the purpose of the school in viewing it in the light of God's purpose for the school in its local community. The head acknowledges that irrespective of whether the head or anyone else is a Christian, or whether it is a Church school or not, God is already present in the school, in its activities and in all the people related to the school. This belief is based on the Biblical revelation of God, *'I am the living God'*.

It becomes exciting to contemplate what 'finding' life means under these circumstances. For contemporary Church of England leaders, in schools and elsewhere, it is a huge test of their faith in Christ, and a challenge to Christians in this country of the meaning of transformation.

Chapter 5

Lessons to be drawn: using free resources

We have learned from these three headteachers how, as the single new ingredient introduced into three failing schools, it is possible for schools to be genuinely turned round. They have shown how to work with the same pupils who have been disruptive, resistant to learning and ready to play truant at the first excuse, leading them to become active agents in their own school's transformation. They have enabled staff who previously had been struggling, suffering from loss of morale and motivation, to take initiatives that made their schools living, vibrant places to which everyone, pupils and teachers, could feel proud to belong. Their schools, having been shunned by parents of 11-year olds, became schools which were able to offer new futures for them.

At heart, this was achieved by those heads being willing to put themselves on the line in the interests of the children in the school. This has not been soft or cosy: they offered tough love to children and to adults. They have not always been popular, but that has been less important to them than working to the very best of their ability in the interests of the school's purpose. This has involved their learning to fully take the role of head – *to be the best head they could*. By so doing they have created the conditions where each child in the school could find their own ways to take their roles: *to be the best pupil they could.* Each teacher learned to manage their own anxieties and stresses, so that they could do the best they could for their pupils, and thus *to be the best teacher they could.* All together, this meant that each school was set on the road to becoming *the best school that it could be*. As any good head would, they felt accountable to the children and their parents, but as followers of Christ they took on these schools as a vocation, which mean that at the end they felt accountable to God for what they did: this did not narrow their sense of accountability, but placed it within an even wider context. It meant that they saw their responsibility as being to make the school *fit for purpose* in rich and long-lasting ways.

We have introduced language and conceptual models to help think about life in schools: the *Reed Rainbow* of human and social interaction; the fundamental concepts of *person, system, context* and *role*. This language is not an imposition on what was going on, but a tool for describing the best of what was actually being done in these schools. The beauty is that the contribution to this language and concepts to understanding how these schools were transformed, are not hugely expensive to put into practice.

Of course money is important, but there are many schools on which fortunes have been spent to little avail. However, *feelings are sources of energy* which, when they are understood, can be directed towards transformation rather than resistance. And they are free!

These heads had the wisdom that was needed to mobilize the feelings present in their school, bringing it round, even against the odds. Their Christian faith was a key factor in how they did that, but much of what they did can be done by men and women who do not share their faith. *Wisdom* is not the exclusive property of the church or of Christians. However, if followers of Christ can offer to others what they can do, drawing on the resources of their faith, then others can find their own ways of making those insights applicable to their own realistic situations.

Appendix: the study method outlined

In studying these three schools we explored different aspects of experience of the schools. We were interested not simply in the recollections of the heads, but in how what they said they had done was reflected in the basic way they worked in the school. So, in a long interview at first, we interviewed them about what they remembered they had done when they arrived: we then met them a further five times at fortnightly intervals in which we explored with them their approach to the issues they were currently handling in the school.

We also interviewed a sample of teachers, support staff, governors and parents about their experience of the transformation and what they saw to be the key factors in how the head had led the school. At the time. We interviewed external figures – local education authority officers, Diocesan Directors of Education and community leaders. We studied documents – prospectuses, minutes of key meetings, head's reports to governors, Panda reports and Ofsted inspection reports.

And of course we interviewed pupils. In two of the schools, we saw the students directly ourselves; but in one school we were able to use a device whereby we worked with a group of pupils who undertook the study with their peers and then reported back to us. This provided us with open and interesting material, raising many questions for us about interview methodologies for the future. In that school, we were also able to meet ex-pupils.

The findings in all three schools showed a consistency of behaviour, attitudes and approach between all three heads which we can now describe.

Notes

1. St Paul's letter to the Christians in Philippi [Philippians 2: 7/8]
2. The diagram is called the Reed Rainbow in recognition of the initial work by the late Bruce Reed in devising it.
3. Attachment Theory has developed to a great extent recently. The new thinking is well summarized in Susan Gerhardt's *Why Love Matters*, Brunner Routledge, Hove, UK, 2004.
4. A study of young volunteers carried out by The Grubb Institute with funds from the Social Science Research Council found that those who offered their time and energy to work voluntarily in the community did so for two, mutually reinforcing reasons. Firstly, they wanted to explore what would make up a part of a world they feel would be fit to live in, for example, a world that cares for persons, or a world where the environment is cared for or a world where respect for a good authority shapes relationships. Secondly, they wished to test out whether or not they can be active contributors to such worlds. See C Quine and J Bazalgette: *The Role of the Young Volunteer*, The Grubb Institute, London, 1978.
5. In conjunction with the Children's Research Centre of the Open University, the Grubb Institute is in the process of designing a radical project to open up new conceptions of pupil leadership; see Chapter 4.

6. These virtues are given particular prominence in Christian thinking and are frequently referred to in St Paul's various letters to Christians in the early churches.
7. H J Nouwen: *The Wounded Healer*, p76 – Darton, Longman and Todd, London UK, 2004.
8. Role theory has been around in sociology and psychology for over a century. The work of The Grubb Institute has been to focus closely and carefully on the interface between person and system. We have defined aspects of that interaction, taking into account the nature of how relations between human beings shape and affect the extent to which the institution can offer them satisfaction and fulfilment through their joint endeavours.
9. For so many of us, size is associated with power or lack of it. This affects life in schools, both for children and staff.
10. We use the definition of 'system' used by Gregory Bateson: activities with a boundary. This differentiates our usage from other definitions which refer to 'procedures', 'protocols' and 'information systems'. This is an important distinction because it keeps in view the fluid nature of human systems, responding to the shifts and changes of both their context and their inner world. It also takes into account the capacity of human systems to resist change – homeostasis as it is called. This perspective opposes the tendency to treat human systems as if they were simply a variation on mechanical systems, which tends to treat human beings as if they were balls on a billiard table, responding to the blow of the billiard cue.
11. Gehardt (2004) op. cit.
12. Eugene Peterson, in his modern translation of the Bible, comments on wisdom. 'Wisdom is the biblical term for this 'on-earth-as-it-is-in heaven' everyday living. Wisdom is the art of living skilfully in whatever actual conditions we find ourselves. It has nothing to do with information as such, knowledge as such.' Eugene Peterson: *The Message:*

The New Testament, Psalms and Proverbs in Contemporary Language, Navpress Publishing Group, Colorado Springs, 1993.

13. Praxis is originally a Greek concept. It refers to the way a person's beliefs and theories are expressed through behaviour. It is through one's praxis that one's true beliefs are manifested. Those who take positions of leadership have nowhere to hide: what they truly hold to be important surfaces, whether they wish it or not, though they may conceal aspects of their personality and actions which they are not proud of, in the end 'the truth will out'.
14. Review Group: *The Way Ahead: Church of England Schools in the New Millennium,* para 3.12 – Church House Publishing, 2001.
15. Bruce Reed: *The Dynamics of Religion,* Darton, Longman and Todd, 1978.
16. The Bloxham Project website describes the Project as seeking to support and challenge schools, Dioceses, LEAs and other educational institutions, and to provide a collective voice of reflective discernment in the educational 'market place' and in the context of our multi-faith society and sometimes conflicting values. Its aims include the desire to: drive forward a spiritually grounded holistic view of educational leadership; and to develop schools' self understandings as places of community and faith.
17. Following Lord Butler's report into the intelligence services' use of evidence in the Iraq crisis, the idea of 'group think' has gained currency. This is similar, but not the same as what we are referring to here since it does not include a sense of the sacred which is associated with 'civil religion'. See *Review of Intelligence on Weapons of Mass Destruction,* (The Butler Report, HMSO, 14 July 2004).
18. Michael Rutter: *Fifteen Thousand Hours: Secondary Schools and their effects upon Children,* p.205, Open Books, London, 1979.
19. BBC website for 17 May 2004.

20. See Government figures quoted in The Independent, 18 August 2004. The four ethnic categories used (White, Black, Asian and Mixed ethnicity) all rated family as most important. The survey also found that black people from the Caribbean and Africa rated it third most important after family and ethnicity/culture, while those from Asian backgrounds rated it second to family. Those of mixed ethnicity rated it seventh.
21. St Paul's letter to the Christians at Colossae [Colossians 4:11].

Glossary

FE (Futher Education) colleges – for adults and students over the age of 16 (and more recently for limited numbers of students aged 14–16). Usually providing vocational education, such as qualifications in plumbing and bricklaying, alongside advanced levels and general national vocational qualifications, pre-degree courses and diplomas, and modules of degree courses under licence from universities.

GCSE – General Certificate of Secondary Education: the examinations set nationally for pupils at the end of Year 11 (aged 16). These examinations usually combine tests set at the end of two years' study with work carried out during the course. Grades range from A* (top grade) to G.

HMI – Her Majesty's Inspectors: people trained to inspect schools but employed directly by Ofsted instead of by the independent contractors who inspect schools and write reports on them. HMI check the inspections that the contractors run.

INSET – In-service training: the professional training and development in which teachers engage whilst they are in full-time work as teachers.

LEA – Local Education Authority: a branch of each city or area's council with responsibility towards the council for the running of schools in the area. Money is given in the form of grants directly from government to each council, which determines (unless directed otherwise by the Chancellor of the Exchequer) what percentage of this grant will be allocated to the LEA. The LEA also has the freedom to determine how much of the grant will be given to its schools; it retains some funds to provide central services, such as advisors for education strategy; personnel functions; payroll services; education psychologists; special educational needs support staff.

Ofsted – Office for Standards in Education: a department of government set up to check that schools, colleges, nurseries etc are providing satisfactory levels of education. Standards are defined in frameworks for inspection, so that everyone acting as an inspector will use them in the same way. Ofsted tries to ensure that the standards set and met are as objective as those set and used by driving test examiners.

PANDA – Performance and Assessment: PANDA reports are sent to each school annually to assist them in self-evaluation, target setting and the development of plans to raise standards. The report is a management tool to help school managers see how effective their school is in comparison with other schools.

SATs – Standard Attainment Tests: nationally set tests in English and Maths for pupils at the end of Year 2 (usually aged 7); Year 6 (aged 11) and Year 9 (aged 14). SATs in Year 9 include tests in Maths and Information and Communications Technology (ICT).

Special Measures – a term used by inspectors when they judge that a school needs direct supervision by Her Majesty's Inspectors and additional resources from the local education authority, for a period of about two years. During this time, the school is visited on a termly basis (or more) by HMI, who decide at what point the school is now functioning well enough to be removed from Special Measures.

About the Authors

Lord Dearing

Lord Dearing served as Chairman and Chief Executive of the Post Office before being called to advise on educational matters.

In 1993 he investigated the National Curriculum for schools which was felt to be overloading teachers and pupils. His report recommended that the Curriculum be slimmed down, so that more time would be available for wider learning and more dynamic teaching.

Following this he was asked to report on Higher Education which he did in 1997. This led to different funding for universities, the expansion of sub-degree and degree courses, and the establishment of training for university teachers.

In 1999 the Archbishop's Council asked him to chair a Review Group on Church of England schools. This Group reported in 2002 in *The Way Ahead*. This report recommended that, in the interest of the wider community's health, the Church of England should set about increasing the number of its secondary provision by the equivalent of 100 schools. This has been the basis on which the Church of England has gone about its policy of expansion, using the present government's policy of setting up independently-sponsored academies as its funding mechanism.

John Bazalgette

When John began teaching in one of the first comprehensive schools in the country he was challenged to draw on his own varied school experience in India, Venezuela and England to enable him to work. Timetabled to teach politics and economics, history, General Studies and religious instruction across the school he had to devise his own way to engage students who ranged from 12-year olds with special needs, barely able to read and write, to the school's first entrants to Oxbridge. After an academic study of education at Exeter, where he worked with Robin Pedley, the guru of comprehensive education, he joined the trust that became The Grubb Institute.

There he undertook the Institute's first action-research project on the relations between young people and adults. This involved, amongst other things, street work in Islington at the time when that area had the highest murder rate in Europe. Drawing on Bruce Reed's experience of the self-governing Lyndhurst Club in Camden, and using the beginning of same conceptual framework which underpins this book, he worked with groups of teenagers for three years. The report on that work, *Freedom, Authority and the Young Adult* (Pitmans Publishing), was published in 1971.

That led to work in Coventry city centre, exploring how young people's experience in school, especially of their working relations with teachers and colleagues, related to what they would find when they got to work. This study was published in 1978 as *School-Life and Work-life in the Inner City* (Hutchinson). This was described by the Careers Research and Advisory Centre as 'trail blazing', raising as it did fundamental questions about the way school organisation affects the emotional learning of children and how that affects their capacity to engage with the adult world beyond school. With Jean and Bruce Reed he was involved in a study of how the UK supported students from overseas. This was published as *Freedom to Study: Requirements of Overseas Students in the UK*, published by the Overseas Students Trust and The Grubb Institute in 1978. This study had a major impact on government policy, and university and college practice in the late 70s and 80s.

Besides work in education John has consulted and researched in business, government agencies, criminal justice agencies and religious bodies (not only Christian ones). He has worked in continental Europe, USA, Ireland and Africa. He is currently piloting a project where 13-year olds in an inner-city comprehensive school are trained in social science research skills with which they investigate issues that their School Council believes will transform their school. These issues are then taken to the school's Leadership Team and Governors to be incorporated into the School Development Programme.

He is married, with five children and nine grandchildren. In his spare time he has been a governor of an inner city comprehensive for over 30 years and has recently been co-opted onto the governing body of a major independent boys school. He is a regular worshipper at his local parish church.

Bruce Reed

Bruce Reed, the founder of the Grubb Institute in 1969, worked as one of the first organisational analysts in the UK until his death in 2003. An Australian, he was ordained in Sydney, and read theology at Cambridge. He opened up new ways of thinking about how theology illuminates our experience, which are central to the conceptual framework which is used in this book. He worked with leaders and managers in all sectors of society in the UK and abroad, particularly with church leaders. Besides his work with school heads and other teachers, he initiated self-government in youth work that led to child-centred practice which has been used widely in places of learning.

Jean Reed

Jean Reed is a senior organisational analyst at the Grubb Institute. She has worked in a wide range of organisations including schools and universities, both in the UK and internationally. For over twenty years she was a school governor in inner London, and chaired a successful amalgamation of two comprehensive schools. She led innovative governor training programmes in a south London borough and took part in designing and undertaking school leadership training, including for the National College for School Leadership. She is a trustee of City YMCA London.

Ian Kehoe

Ian Kehoe graduated from University College Dublin with a Master's Degree in Philosophy and then went on to work in The Grubb Institute for three years as a Research Officer. While there, his work focused on issues relating to children's inclusion and participation and included work for the Department for Education and Skills' BEST Development Programme, NCSL, and Cambridge University's Pembroke House. He is currently researching and writing a book on systemic approaches to transforming school bullying.

Jill Clough

Jill Clough is an experienced headteacher and an Associate of The Grubb Institute. She focuses on child-centred practice: how adults interact with young people rather than acting on their behalf. She is a mentor and coach for headteachers, groups of schools, and teams of staff, on behalf of organisations such as the Association of School and College Leaders and the National College for School Leadership. She writes about the creativity of leadership, and how schools might transform themselves through their vision of human potential, not just through evaluation.

For details of her book *Why (Some) State Schools Fail ...* see inside back cover.

The Grubb Institute

The Grubb Institute was set up in 1969 to contribute to the well-being and wholeness of society by enabling persons, communities and institutions to transform to meet real human need.

Everywhere, every day, we see evidence of damage to human life and the environment. Not only the sustainability of our environment but the sustainability of the social fabric of our families, communities, institutions and wider societies is in question. The overwhelming evidence suggests that the current status quo is unsustainable.

The critical challenge humanity faces is how we can individually and corporately take responsibility for the world we have contributed to creating.

The Institute and those associated with it believe humanity needs to transform itself and that to do this we need to challenge radically and actively the way we live together as human beings.

Over forty years of working at the pressure points of society as researchers and consultants, tells us that when human beings of whatever age can find purpose, they can transform and use their full capacities in the systems that they create together. Through offering specialist skills, Institute staff seek to gather and work with concerned people in creating the conditions for a sustainable, humane and inclusive world – what can be understood as God's creation – where people can deal with suffering, hate, selfishness, and greed, and live by the values of justice, forgiveness, service, respect and love.

Using expertise developed from the human sciences and applied theology, the Institute offers consultancy and action research to education, health, social care, religious and voluntary organisations, and businesses. The Institute has a Christian Council, while staff and associates come from a range of faith and spiritual positions and work with persons, groups and organisations whatever their beliefs may be.

The Grubb Institute
Cloudesley Street
London N1 0HU
UK

Website: www.grubb.org.uk

Index

Abraham, 55
accountability to governors, 34
accountability, mutual, 140
achievement, raising, 82
acquiring values, 45
act of worship, *see* daily worship
activities, system of, 112
adult child interactions, 69
adulthood, growth to, 69
aim, school, 110
ambition tree, 79
anger, 144
Anglican schools, some sectarian, 43
anxiety about learning, 76
anxiety, head, 19
appointing new head, 3
assembly, 133
  binds school, 129
  leadership, 128–137
  preparation for, 46
  purpose, 135
  staff behaviour in, 60
  worship and, 45, 58, 128–137
  worship, differ, 64, 135
atheist question, 47
Attachment Theory, 155
attendance record, schools in study, 8, 44
authority, 89
  in practice, 95
  power and, 90–97
  transformation, and, 88–97
baby's experience, 102
baby, belonging, experience, 74
Bateson, Gregory, 156
Bazalgette, John, 155
BBC survey, 148, 157
behaviour
  disciplined, 85
  learning from, 57
  learning, and, 82
  role and, 119
being the head, 50
belonging, 7–65, 73, 74, 80
  at risk, 65
  baby's experience, 74
  boundary and, 107
  corporate, 74
  effects of, 44–50
  family, to, 74
  fundamental to human, 74
  groups, to, 74
  initiation and, 73
  ownership and, 143
  pupils, enabling, 140
  rooted in reality, 49
  school, to, 12–65
  transformation and, 142
  worship and sense of, 61
best possible head, pupils, etc., 152
Bible, 124
Bion, Wilfred, 129
blame culture and truth, 24

Bloxham Conference, 129
Bloxham Project, 157
Bloxham Project Newsletter, 130
boundary, 107, 113
boundary and belonging, 107
buildings, 1, 9, 25, 35, 49, 82, 108
  as message, 48
  civil religion and, 131
  new, pride and, 48
Butler report, 157

candles at staff induction, 60
care of pupils, 13
career, effect on new heads', 20, 21, 62
career, pupils envisioning, 79
Carlson, Jan, 140
cathedral Provost, 91
cathedral, building a, 140
ceremonies, initiation, 70
challenges, 45
  faith, of, 127
  fear of, after failure, 30
  positive response, 30
change versus transformation, 12
change, managing, and leadership, 25
change, resistance to, 25
chaplain, 40, 41, 45, 56, 58, 62, 95
child
  adult, interactions, 69
  becoming adult, 68, 70
  equipping for adulthood, 68
  fostering growth, 69
  sense of adventure, 71
Children's Research Centre, 145, 155
choir schools, 69
Christian faith of new heads, 53
Christian leader, 82, 83, 120
Christian symbols in worship, 58
Christian worship, *see* worship
church involvement, 85
Church of England
  Dearing Review Group, 148
  Established Church, 149
  ethos, 56
  guidance from, 56
  inclusiveness, 123
  other faiths, and, 148
  serve whole population, 42, 43, 55
church policies, local, 43
church schools
  ethos, 33, 40, 59
  exclusive?, 110
  fear of, 9
  Reed Rainbow, 80
  religion imposed?, 61
  transformation, 81
civil religion, 132–134, 136, 157
  buildings and, 131
  defined, 131
  faith and, 134
  head, 136
  inclusiveness and, 132
  key functions, 132
  schools values, 134
  schools, in, 134
  staff, and, 132
classroom learning, 143
Commonwealth Education Ministers, 144
community
  involvement, 85
  leaders, 56
  local, 50
  school and, 24
  school as, 46
  school contribution to, 39
  support of, 85
  transformation, involved, 37, 39
  uniform, approval of, 39
concept
  context, 114–118
  person, 101–107

role, 118–122
system, 107–113
concern for pupils, 56
confidence, of outsiders, 141
consultation by new heads, 25
consultation, staff, 92
context, 113
concept, 114–118
school, 110
corporate belonging, 74
corporate entity, school, 112
corporateness and prayers, 46
corporateness, effect on pupils, 46
creator, God as, 124–126
culture, 84
culture of individualism, 99
culture, no-blame, 21, 24
culture, truth, 24
curriculum syllabus conflict, 123

daily worship, 130
legal requirement, 57
Dearing Report, 123
Dearing Review Group, 148, 157
despair, 144
difficulties, acknowledging, 146
Diocesan Director of Education, 40
Diocesan schools adviser, 56
diocese, 141
demotivated, 39
resources from, 42
responsibility, 39
school, relationship, 39
disadvantaged community
schools in study, 9
discipline and worship, 61
disciplined behaviour, 85
doing things right, 52
drivers of transformation, 88–97
Dynamics of Religion, 129, 157

Economic & Social Research
Council, 145
education
defined, 72
faith and, 53
learning and, 73, 74
Reed Rainbow, 73, 74
Education Act, 1944, 130
empowerment, *see also* maturation, 144
governors, 34, 36
maturation and, 73, 76
staff, 30
enablement, staff, 151
energy, feelings and, 152
enrichment of pupils, 45
envisioning career, pupils, 79
envisioning, transformation and, 73, 79
Established Church, C of E, 149
ethnicity and family, 157
ethnicity and inclusiveness, 123
ethos
Church of England, 56
church school, 33, 40, 59
group, 131
school, 46, 54, 84, 131–134, 144
evangelize, new heads didn't, 4
exam results, *see* GCSE results
exclusion rates, schools in study, 44
exclusive intake, 110, 123
experience, 98, 146
baby's, 102
learning from, 98
experiential power, 90, 106, 119

failing school, effect on staff, 29
faith
challenge for head, 127
civil religion and, 134
commitment of new heads, 11
education and, 53
new heads, 89

no objections to, 55
openness and, 62
should be private?, 55, 94
Faith Development Centre, 59
family, 69, 70
belonging to, 74
ethnicity and, 157
faults as incentive to improve, 50
FE (Futher Education) colleges, 159
fear of challenges after failure, 30
fear of church schools, 9
feelings and energy, 152
feelings, mobilizing, 152
Fifteen Thousand Hours, 157
finding the role, 84
fit for Kingdom, 127
fit for purpose, 139, 152
focus on pupils, governors', 36
focus, what matters, 82
food, playing with, 72
forgiveness, 17
Free Church, new heads, 10, 55, 124
freedom and worship, 61
Fresh Start, 25, 26

GCSE, 159
GCSE results
other successes, 143
schools in study, 4, 8, 44, 46, 47, 142
generations
tensions between, 71
transferring knowledge, 68
Gerhardt, Susan, 102, 103, 155, 156
God
creator, as, 124–126
grace, reliance, 82
human accountability to, 81
king & judge, as, 124, 126
kingdom, school as, 126
love of, 64
new heads experience of, 17
providence, 81
purpose, 21, 85, 149
redeemer, as, 124, 126
sustainer, as, 124
tough love, 15
transcendent, 124
vision, interpreting, 29
Gospel challenge to ethos, 134
government policy, 144
governors
belonging to school, 24
development of, 147
empowerment, 34, 36
experience of schools, 36
head's frankness with, 36
heads accountable to, 34
heads' reliance on, 34
inclusiveness, 148
motivation, 34
parents, 37
potential splits, 37
pupils as primary focus, 36
teachers, 37
grace, 11, 23, 47, 77, 126
grace, reliance on, 82
graffiti, 49, 82
grammar schools, 69
groups, belonging to, 74
Grubb Institute, 86, 100, 155, 156

head
anxiety, 19
appointing new, 3
being the, 50
best possible, 152
civil religion, 136
governors, frankness with, 36
holistic picture, 80
key task, 134
new, *see* new heads
open door policy, 29

parachuting in new, 3, 97
person, as, 105, 106, 112
proselytizing?, 94
respect, earning, 29
sensitivity to staff feelings, 28
spirit of service of, 28
staff, relationship, 96
staff, respect for, 17
super, 3, 11
understanding needs, 20
Her Majesty's Inspectors
(of Schools), *see* inspections
holistic picture, head's, 80
Holy Communion, 65
honest mistakes, 22
honesty, new heads, 36
hope, 24, 82
staff, 30
human accountability to God, 81
human interaction, model of, 68
human interaction, Reed Rainbow, 70
humility, new heads, 28, 36, 48

ideas-in-the-mind, 100, 109, 111, 118
identity, 45
inwardness of, 45
outwardness of, 45
immanent, 124
implications
leadership, 106, 113, 114, 121, 127
management, 106, 113, 114, 121, 127
power, 89
incarnation of Jesus, 29
inclusive intake, 110, 148
inclusiveness, 43, 44, 56, 124, 127
belief, of, 55
Church of England, 123
civil religion, and, 132
diversity recognized, 62
gift and challenge, 148–150
gift to society, as, 123–127
governors, 148
leadership, 146
not recognized, 110
principle, 148
reflects population ethnicity, 123
society, 62
worship, 62
Independent, The, 157
individualism, culture of, 99
initiation
belonging and, 73
ceremonies, 70
defined, 72, 73
Reed Rainbow, 73
inner world, 101, 102, 112, 115, 156
INSET, 159
inspections, 8, 159
institution
in-the-mind, 109, 110, 112, 114
religion, in, 130
specific existence, 109
understanding the, 84
instrumental power, 92
intake
changed, 3, 10
Christian, proportion, 9
covert criteria, 44
exclusive, 110, 123
inclusive, 110, 148
multi-faith, 40
Muslim, 9, 45
profile, 9
selective, 43
Sikh, 9
unchanged, 3, 8, 10, 82
intentions, new heads, 81
Inter-faith Centre, 45
interviews for study, staff, 153
investment as symbol, 48
involvement, outsider, 85
inwardness of identity, 45

iterative process, role, 86

Jesus, incarnation, 29
Jourdain, Monsieur, 120

king & judge, God, 124, 126
Kingdom, fit for, 127

language of Reed Rainbow, 81, 152
language spoken, schools in study, 9
LEA, 85, 141, 159
leadership
  assembly, 128–137
  based on reality, 28
  community, 56
  from anywhere, 81
  implications, 106, 113, 114, 121, 127
  inclusiveness, 146
  managing change, 25
  person, of, 68–97
  principles, 67–137
  pupil, *see* pupil leadership
  pupils, by, 144
  pupils, of, 142
  servant, 29
  spiritual task, 128
  staff, of, 85
  systems, managing, 97–122
  transformation, 81
  transformation and, 122–128
  worship, 128–137
league tables, 76
learning
  anxiety about, 76
  behaviour and, 82
  behaviour, from, 57
  broader, 143
  classroom, 143
  education and, 73, 74
  experience, from, 98
  partnership, benefits of, 75
  teaching, contrasted, 78
  worship and, 57
legal requirement, daily worship, 57
listening to pupils, 19
literacy, schools in study, 9
local communities, 50
Local Educational Authority, *see* LEA
longevity of transformation, 47, 97
love irrespective of faith, 61
love of God, 64

making the role, 84–86
management discussion, 108
management implications, 106, 113, 114, 121, 127
managing school structure, 85
managing sub-systems, 112
managing zone, 105
maturation, 130
  affects all, 77
  defined, 72
  empowerment and, 73, 76
  opportunity, 144
  power and, 77
  Reed Rainbow, 73, 76
  Sebastian, 78
  tutor groups, 77
media, 141
media criticism of schools, 9, 10
mental constructs, 100, 109
Message, The, 156
messages, symbolic, 13
mistakes
  dealing with, 21, 53
  honest, 22
  learning from, 24
  reality and, 21
mobilizing processes, 141
model
  human interaction, of, 68
  social development, of, 68

tribal chief, 116
Moliere, 120
morale, low staff, 4, 9, 12, 31, 151
motivation
governors, 34
new heads, 20, 81, 142
staff, 85
multi-directional relationships, 64
multi-faith, intake, 40
Muslim, intake, 9, 45
mutual accountability, 140
mutual encouragement of staff, 31
mutual support
pupils, 79
staff, 30

naming and shaming schools, 2
National College for School Leadership, 147
negatives, dealing with, 144
networks, school as, 112
new heads
accountable to governors, 34
behaviour, perception of, 55
benefiting school, 50, 86
career, effect on, 20, 21, 62
commitment to faith, 11
common factors, 10
consulted widely, 25
effectiveness, 50
evangelizing, not, 4
experience of God, 17
faith, 53, 89
faith, no objections, 55
faith, parents' perception, 34
faith, pupils' approval, 60
faith, staff perception, 32
forgiveness, 17
Free Church, 10, 55, 124
honesty, 36
humility, 28, 36, 48
intentions, 81
interpreting God's vision, 29
leadership, *see* leadership
local church policies, 43
love, 15
motivation, 20, 81, 142
move away?, 21
new life, awareness of, 17
non-Anglican, 10, 55
parent partnership, 32
parents' belief in, 32
performance evaluation, 81, 82
professionalism, 11, 56, 89
reliance on governors, 34
Roman Catholic, 10, 55, 124
special mission, 4
staff, belief in, 32
transformation, and, 10
valuing pupils, 15
vocation, 21, 152
whole school approach, 30
'new life', 17
new replacement staff, 3, 10, 29
New Visions, 147
no-blame culture, 21, 24
non-Anglican new heads, 55
Nouwen, Henry J, 83, 120, 156
numeracy, schools in study, 9

official power, 91
Ofsted, 2, 4, 7, 8, 10, 35, 37, 46, 57, 82, 84, 114, 126, 139, 153, 160
old-fashioned teaching, 76
open door policy of head, 29
Open University, 145, 155
openness and faith, 62
operating systems, 112
opus Dei, 124, 127
organization, 110
in-the-mind, 109, 110, 112, 114
transformation, 143

oscillation theory, 129, 136
other faiths, CofE and, 148
outer world, 101, 102
outside agencies, working with, 40
outsiders, confidence of, 141
outwardness of identity, 45
over-subscribed, school, 4
ownership and belonging, 143

P+p, *see* projected power, positive
P-p, *see* projected power, negative
PANDA, 160
parachuting in new head, 3, 97
parents
  belonging to school, 24
  education not valued, 34
  governors, 37
  involvement, 85
  new heads, belief in, 32
  new heads, partnerships with, 32
  pride in school, 48
  problems handling children, 34
  shared purpose, 32
  transformation, role in, 32
parish church, 58, 60
partnership in learning, 75
Pentonville Prison, 143
performance evaluation, new heads, 81, 82
person
  concept, 101–107
  head as, 105, 106, 112
  power as attribute, 89
  shape of, 77
personal boundary, 102
personal transformation, 143
Peterson, Eugene, 156
pew fodder, 42
physical power and maturation, 77
Pi, *see* instrumental power
playing with food, 72
Po, *see* official power
power
  authority and, 90–97
  defined, 89
  experiential, *see* experiential power
  five types, 90–95
  implications of, 89
  in practice, 95
  instrumental, *see* instrumental power
  official, *see* official power
  projected, *see* projected power
  spiritual, *see* spiritual power
  transformation, and, 88–97
Pp, *see* projected power
practical, value-laden versus, 51
praxis, 120, 121, 146, 157
prayers, corporateness and, 46
prayers, staff meetings, 46, 55
preaching and worship, 57
prefects, 144
Press, *see* media
pride
  in school, 48
  new buildings, 48
  not lying, 50
  prize-giving, 48, 93
Prison, Pentonville, 143
prize-giving, pride at, 48, 93
processes, school, 110
professional experience, 69
professionalism, new heads, 11, 56, 89
projected power, 93
  negative, 93, 106
  positive, 93, 106, 117
proselytizing by heads?, 94
Provost, cathedral, 91
Ps, *see* spiritual power
psychic skin, 102
psychological power and maturation, 77
psychological role, 119

pupil leadership, 81, 142–146
  preparation, 145
  teachers and, 145
pupils
  belonging, enabling, 140
  best possible, 152
  care of, 13
  career, envisioning, 79
  concern for, 56
  corporateness, effect of, 46
  enrichment of, 45
  governors' primary focus, 36
  head's faith, approval, 60
  leadership, *see* pupil leadership
  leadership by, 144
  leadership of, 142
  listening to, 19
  love, new heads, 15
  mutual support, 79
  needs, understanding of, 20
  participation, 144
  respect, 18
  safety experienced by, 19
  self-belief, 142
  self-esteem, 97
  sensitivity to, 85
  social responsibility of, 80
  transformation and, 151
  valued by new heads, 15
purpose of school, 84
Px, *see* experiential power

Quine, Colin, 155

racism, 93
RE, *see* religious education
reality and mistakes, 21
reality and truth, 21
reality of life, 126
reality, facing problems, 36
reality, leadership based on, 28
redeemer, God as, 124, 126
redemption, 125
Reed Rainbow, 141, 155
  church schools, 80
  education, 73, 74
  human interaction, of, 70
  initiation, 73
  language, provides, 81, 152
  maturation, 73, 76
  practical application, 81
  social development, of, 70
  transformation, 73, 79
Reed, Bruce, 129, 136, 155, 157
religare, 129
religion
  civil, *see* civil religion
  institutions, in, 130
  oscillation theory, 129
  schools, in, 131
  transcended, 126
religious education, 45, 55–57
  worship, differ, 56
removing existing staff, 3
reputation, 84
reputation, fragility, 39
resources, 84, 85, 114
  extra finance, 25
respect, head earning, 29
rituals, 68, 131
role
  behaviour and, 119
  concept, 118–122
  defined, 83
  finding the, 84
  iterative process, 86
  making the, 84–86
  psychological, 119
  sailor analogy, 118
  self-discipline and, 83–88
  sociological, 119
  taking the, 86–88

working in, 83, 119
role theory, 156
Roman Catholic
discipline of consistency, 56
new heads, 10, 55, 124
ruffled feathers, staff, 26
Rutter, Michael, 131, 157

safety experienced by pupils, 19
sailor role analogy, 118
SAS, 140
SATs, 160
saying sorry, 17
school
activities, 110
aim, 110
assembly, *see* assembly
belonging to, 12–65
belonging, adults, 24
best possible, 152
chaplain, *see* chaplain
child growth, fostering, 71
choir, 69
civil religion, 134
community and, 24
community, as, 46
community, contribution to, 39
context, 110
corporate entity, 112
diocese, relationship, 39
ethos, *see* ethos, school
God's kingdom, 126
God's purpose, 149
grammar, 69
inclusive, *see* inclusiveness
intake, *see* intake
invented institution, as, 69
naming and shaming, 2
networks, as, 112
pride in, 48
processes, 110
purpose of, 84
religion in, 131
reputation, fragile, 39
structure, managing, 85
success, broader, 143
system, as, 107
uniform, *see* uniform
School Action Plan, 145
school councils, 144
school meals, free, 9
schools in study, 3
achievements, 8
attendance record, 8, 44
Christian intake, 9
disadvantaged community, 9
exclusion rates, 44
GCSE results, 4, 8, 44, 46, 47, 142
history, 7
improvements, 8
media criticism, 9, 10
respect, pupils, 18
roll, 8
self-esteem, 18
self-worth, 18
statistics, 7, 9
transfer to diocese, 7
Sebastian, 75, 76, 78, 79
sectarian, Anglican schools, some, 43
selective intake, 43
self-belief, pupils, 142
self-confidence, staff, 31
self-discipline, 48
role, and, 83–88
self-esteem, pupils, 97
self-esteem, schools in study, 18
self-esteem, staff, 31
self-management, 103
self-worth, schools in study, 18
sense of belonging, *see* belonging
sense of identity, *see* identity
sensitivity to pupils, 85

September 11th, 36, 57, 63, 80
servant leadership, 29
service sub-systems, 112
shape of person, 77
Sikh, 95
  intake, 9
skin, psychic, 102
skin, weak, 105
social development, model of, 68
social development, Reed Rainbow, 70
social responsibility and worship, 80
social responsibility of pupils, 80
Social Science Research Council, 155
sociological role, 119
sorry, saying, 17
Special Measures, 4, 7, 25, 31, 35, 95, 139, 160
spirit of service of head, 28
spiritual power, 94
St Paul's letters, 155, 156, 158
staff
  assembly, behaviour in, 60
  civil religion, and, 132
  consultation, 92
  empowerment, 30
  enablement, 151
  existing, 'doing favour', 26
  failing school's effect on, 29
  head's faith, perception, 32, 34
  head, relationship, 96
  hope, 30
  induction, candles at, 60
  interviews for study, 153
  leadership of, 85
  long-serving, 9
  low morale, 4, 9, 12, 31, 151
  manipulation perceived, 29
  motivation, 85
  mutual encouragement of, 31
  mutual support, 30
  new heads belief in, 32
  new replacement, 3, 10, 29
  no new, 25
  not devalued, 82
  not working with, 29
  potential, 29
  removing existing, 3
  resentment possible, 26
  respect from head, 17
  ruffled feathers, 26
  self-confidence, 31
  self-esteem, 31
  sensitivity of head, 28
  unchanged, 3, 8, 10, 82
  worship and, 60, 62
staff meetings
  prayers, 46, 55
  thought for the day, 62
strategies for success, 44
study
  authors' background, 68
  interviews, 153
  method, 153
sub-systems, managing, 112
success, strategies for, 44
super head, 3, 11
survey, BBC, 148, 157
sustainer, God as, 124
syllabus curriculum conflict, 123
symbol, investment as, 48
symbols, 13
synergy, 141
system, 113
  activities, of, 112
  Bateson definition, 156
  concept, 107–113
  experiencing, 109
  managing, 97–122
  operating, 112
  school as, 107

taking the role, 86–88

targets, 44, 46
Tavistock, 129
teachers, *see also* staff
  belonging to school, 24
  best possible, 152
  governors, 37
  pupil leadership, and, 145
teaching
  learning, contrasted, 78
  old-fashioned, 76
That'll Teach 'Em, 76
That'll Teach 'Em Too, 76
'them and us', 107
thought for the day, 58, 62, 63
  staff meetings, 62
toilets, 82
  condition, as symbol, 92
  trashed, 22, 92
tough love, God's, 15
tough love, heads', 151
transcendent, God, 124
transcending religion, 126
transformation
  action programme, 139, 146
  authority, and, 88–97
  belonging and, 142
  care insufficient for, 13
  change, compared, 12
  church school-specific, 81
  community involvement, 37, 39
  concepts, 146
  cooperation, spirit of, 52
  creating new ties, 37
  defined, 12, 72
  drive, 88–97
  envisioning and, 73, 79
  expensive in time, 147
  head as single new factor, 10, 25
  leadership, 81
  leadership in, 122–128
  longevity of, 47, 97
  new head, 10
  organization, 143
  others involved in, 37, 39
  owned by all, 47
  parents' role in, 32
  personal, 143
  power and, 88–97
  pupil leadership, 142–146
  pupils and, 151
  pupils' vision, and, 79
  Reed Rainbow, 73, 79
  school over-subscribed, 4
  self-questioning, 135
  values percolated, 47
  whole culture, 142
tribal chief model, 116
tribe, 69
trust, 88
truth, 24
truth and reality, 21
truth culture, 24
truth, blame culture and, 24
truth, working with, 22
tutor groups, 46, 60, 62, 112
  maturation, 77
Twin Towers, *see* September 11th

unexpected energy, 72, 79
uniform, 19, 45, 48, 49, 82, 92, 131, 132
  community approval of, 39
  head paid for, 15
  new, as message, 48
universal schooling, 69
'us and them', 107

value-laden versus practical, 51
values, acquiring, 45
values, percolating, 47
vicious circle, 1–5, 96, 132
village, 69
village, African saying, 69

virtuous circle, initiating, 3
vision
    developing, 143
    tapping into, 79
    widened, 61
vocation, new heads, 21, 152

Way Ahead, The, 157, 161
weak skin, 105
Weapons of Mass Destruction, Review, 157
whole school approach, 30
Why Love Matters, 155, 156
wisdom, 105, 152
wisdom, deepest, 125
wise heads, formation, 146
working in role, 83, 119
worship, 45
    all participated, 62
    assembly and, 58, 128–137
    assembly, differ, 64, 135
    belonging, sense of, 61
    broadening effect of, 62
    central importance, 57–65
    Christian symbols in, 58
    daily, *see* daily worship
    discipline and, 61
    freedom and, 61
    key school activity, 58, 141
    leadership, 128–137
    leading, shared, 60
    opening minds, 62
    preaching and, 57
    RE differs, 56
    significance, 127
    social responsibility and, 80
    spirit of, 60
    staff and, 60, 62
    staff behaviour in, 60
    whole-school, 55
Wounded Healer, The, 156

Youth Summit, 144

zone, managing, 105

ALSO PUBLISHED BY UIT CAMBRIDGE LTD.

The Idealogical Battle for Education

A History of Political Influence on Schools

Rt. Hon. Dame Angela Rumbold

Angela Rumbold was Minister for Education from 1986 to 1990 and has continued to be actively involved in schools. She is now Chairman of the United Learning Trust, currently setting up 16 City Academies for the Government. Her controversial book examines the effect of politics on education:

- The early history of political involvement in educating all children, in particular those who couldn't afford to pay for a public school.
- The increasing importance of education as a social tool for politicians, and the conflicts between the educationalists and the politicians.
- The ideological battle that developed in the mid 20th Century, starting with the 1944 Butler Act. Since then, much energy has been spent on structural changes to schools, curriculum and examinations.

The book takes a long hard look at the result of all this change, arguing that much of the debate has devalued the professional delivery of education in the classroom, and so has contributed to the disengagement of pupils in their own pursuit of knowledge.

The book ends with a discussion on the disadvantages of teaching for employment, as against educating young people to allow them to continue learning throughout their lives.

ISBN: 978-0-9544529-4-0
Publication date: 2007

ALSO PUBLISHED BY UIT CAMBRIDGE LTD.

Why State Schools Fail

Dr Jill Clough

This book supports state schools. It examines why so many are failing in Britain today; in particular, why do some schools fail, when many state and independent schools are excellent? What can we do to give all our children the education they need?

Jill Clough moved from a successful career as head in independent schools, to take over a failing sink school, and after only three terms the school was taken out of Special Measures. This book tells the story and analyzes how state schools can offer the benefits usually associated with independent schools.

I would advise anyone who cares about education to read and consider this touching and important book. **Jilly Cooper**

Beautifully written ... a moving story ... shows how petty bureaucracy can deprive needy children of the benefits of innovative leadership – it provides essential reading for those who believe in bringing the two sectors of education together in this country

Rt. Hon. Dame Angela Rumbold
Former Senior Minister of State for Education

ISBN: 0-9544529-1-7

Available from good bookshops or direct from the publishers.

For more information about our books on schools,
or to be added to our mailing list see:
www.uit.co.uk
or e-mail **inquiries@uit.co.uk**
or call +44 1223 302 041